D1566454

Cass Gilbert

The Early Years

CASS GILBERT

The Early Years

GEOFFREY BLODGETT

MINNESOTA
HISTORICAL
SOCIETY
PRESS

Publication of this book was supported, in part, with funds provided by the June D. Holmquist Publication Endowment Fund of the Minnesota Historical Society.

www.mnhs.org/mhspress

Manufactured in the United States of America

10 9 8 7 6 5 4 3 2 1

♾ The paper used in this publication meets the minimum requirements of the American National Standard for Information Sciences—Permanence for Printed Library Materials, ANSI Z39.48-1984

International Standard Book Number
0-87351-410-6 (cloth)

Library of Congress Cataloging-in-Publication Data

Blodgett, Geoffrey.
Cass Gilbert : the early years / Geoffrey Blodgett.
p. cm.
Includes bibliographical references and index.
ISBN 0-87351-410-6 (cloth : alk. paper)
1. Gilbert, Cass, 1859–1934.
2. Architects—Minnesota—Biography.
3. Architects—United States—Biography.
I. Title.

NA737.G5 B58 2001
720'.92—dc21
[B] 2001031577

Title pages: Cass Gilbert on roof of Minnesota State Capitol, 1901.

For Jane Blodgett
And our three daughters
Lauren Sharpe
Barbara Blodgett
Sally Olson

Acknowledgments

The following people have made important contributions to the quality of the tale told in these pages. Their names also appear where appropriate in the body of the text and notes.

Roland Baumann, Tom Blanck, Norman C. Craig, Jan Forsberg, Ellen Fridinger, Dewey Ganzel, Hugh Huestler, Sharon Irish, Paul Clifford Larson, Robert Longsworth, Pat Murphy, Shannon Pennefeather, Franz Schulze, Sandra Slater, Jean Tierney, Marilyn Vogel, Richard Guy Wilson.

Cass Gilbert: The Early Years

Introduction

One night in the mid-1890s Cass Gilbert paused in his architectural work to copy a Ben Franklin adage into his diary. "The sleeping fox catches no poultry," Franklin reminded him. Pungent and brief, the thought had special urgency at that moment in Gilbert's career. It captured his desire, against tough odds, to grasp the definitive professional success that had thus far eluded him. His ambition was sleepless, and it was soon vindicated. In October 1895 Gilbert's design won the competition for the new Minnesota State Capitol in St. Paul.[1]

This victory brought a satisfying climax to the Minnesota decades of his young career, which began in 1876 with his first apprenticeship in St. Paul. He landed the state capitol commission of 1895 after a long and tortuous effort to ground himself in the local architectural competition. It propelled him to sudden fame and poised him for departure a few years later from St. Paul for New York and a grand entry onto the national stage of his profession. For the balance of his career, until his death in 1934, he was renowned as the most prolific and stylistically versatile architect of his generation, his skills ranging from the picturesque through Beaux-Arts neoclassicism to the new art of the high tower, which culminated in the stunning Woolworth skyscraper of 1913. Moreover, in the early years of the new century he moved into leadership of the country's central architectural establishment. This hierarchical cluster linked Gilbert and his professional colleagues with their most important clients, the monied social elite of urban America, to provide a trusting nation with authoritative aesthetic and cultural guidance. Gilbert believed deeply in the integrity of the stratified social structure underlying the country's architectural establishment. He had worked hard early on to adapt his career to the St. Paul version of this hierarchy, and in New York he finally mastered it. The rough struggle of the Minnesota years proved to be splendid preparation for his later fame.

In 1914 the Great War began, the most important event in American architectural history since the Chicago World's Fair of 1893. From the shock of world war, and the grim void of its aftermath, an iconoclastic new mood called the "modern" emerged. It surfaced more swiftly in Europe, where its origins were grounded in deeper prewar yearnings and the force of the war was vastly more immediate than in America, but when and where it arrived it seemed inexorable. The modern atmosphere, freed by the war's pulverizing impact on so many prewar cultural assumptions, gathered a broad new postwar audience of rebels and seekers—friends of Stravinsky in music, Dos Passos and Hemingway in literature, Watson and Freud in psychology, Picasso in art, Gropius and the Bauhaus in architecture. The salient attitudes of architectural modernism—nonhierarchical, undeferential, "starting from zero"—threatened to wreck Gilbert's career. Suddenly the architecture he had practiced in both St. Paul and New York, mixing Beaux-Arts classicism with the picturesque, seemed overtaken. Almost everything he loved about his craft, and his pride in his contributions to it, were contested by the surge of the modern. Its arrival turned him into an architectural and cultural conservative, a citizen at bay, resisting all the newness of the 1920s. The conservatism he clung to till his death in 1934 combined with the triumph of the modern to send his posthumous reputation into several decades of dark eclipse.

The dark would endure as long as the mood of the modern commanded its audience, across the years between the two world wars, and well past midcentury. Then, beginning in the 1960s, a rival gathering of attitudes, turning on the term "postmodern," took hold. By promoting fresh curiosity about the architectural past, which the modernists thought they had discredited and transcended, postmodernism revived some sympathy, however quirky and ironic, for bygone traditionalists like Cass Gilbert. The dappled sunlight of selective nostalgia now brightened his legacy, and by the end of the century his reputation glowed again.

Testing the value of his legacy and the boundaries of his reputation—his buildings, their meaning, their worth—requires a durable context within which judgments can be cast. The ongoing frenzy in the pace of change among late twentieth-century architectural priorities, and the discordant rivalry among them, soon turned the postmodern persuasion itself into a transient phase, awaiting its own deconstruction and displacement. Fresh stylistic enthusiasms, including even a revival of the once-discredited classical tradition, tumbled after one another almost yearly. These ongoing kaleidoscopic shifts provided no sure backdrop against which to understand architectural decisions reached a century earlier. Therefore an evaluation of Gilbert's legacy can best begin not by trying to measure his career against some arbitrary code of current assumptions and preferences, but rather by examining the structure of the past, now long since vanished, which he entered at birth in the middle of the nineteenth century.

Cass Gilbert, 1880.
(MHS Collections)

Cass Gilbert

The Early Years

1

BEGINNINGS

Cass Gilbert's life began in small-town Midwestern America on the eve of Civil War. He was born in Zanesville, in the gently rolling hill country of southeastern Ohio, on November 24, 1859. His parents' home, while shunning ostentation, was a household of committed strivers. The Gilberts were driven by pride in family status, a preoccupation the growing boy absorbed early on. He was named after a prominent great uncle on his father's side, Lewis Cass, whose long public career had included cabinet posts under Andrew Jackson and James Buchanan, a ministry to France, and a run for the presidency as the Democratic Party nominee in 1848. Lewis Cass had practiced law and served as a federal marshal in Zanesville at the outset of his political career, and the townspeople were very proud of him. The day would come, however, when Zanesville touted more highly the architect born there than the politician who once practiced there.[1]

Cass Gilbert's parents grew up in Zanesville, their families ranked among the town's more prominent citizens. "My people while not rich were always in good circumstances," Gilbert remembered. In middle age he came to enjoy tracking family genealogy and occasionally indulged in a harmless embellishment here and there. He discovered to his great satisfaction that his father was descended from early English migrants to Connecticut—"founders," he called them. He had them arriving in Connecticut in 1618, some fifteen years before that colony was actually settled. Four or five generations later, when the outcome of the American Revolution opened up the trans-Appalachian West for American occupation beginning in the 1780s, Gilbert's grandfather joined the New England migration to Ohio and settled in Zanesville. His son Samuel, Cass Gilbert's father, married Elizabeth Wheeler, the neighboring daughter of a prosperous Zanesville coal mine owner. Cass was the second of their three surviving sons.[2]

Not much is known of Samuel Gilbert's career before or after his marriage to Elizabeth. Cass later told a prospective client, Henry Churchill King, president of Oberlin College in northern Ohio, that his father had attended Oberlin, but there is no other evidence for that statement. While still a young man, Samuel began profiting nicely from family real estate investments in and around Zanesville. Meanwhile, he joined the U.S. Coast Survey and was working as a surveyor, mostly along the Gulf Coast, when Cass was born in 1859. The son did not see his father very often. Samuel Gilbert fought as an officer with the 44th Ohio Volunteer Infantry in the Civil War during Cass's early years; when the war ended, he took off for South America on boundary survey work. Shortly after returning, Samuel Gilbert journeyed to St. Paul, Minnesota, to invest in its flourishing urban land boom and to restore his poor health, a problem left over from the war. His wife and three sons, Charlie, Cass, and Sam, remained at the family home called "The Pines," just outside Zanesville.[3]

Cass Gilbert's mother, Elizabeth Wheeler Gilbert, was a strong, self-sufficient, and commanding woman. Her lineage reached back to eighteenth-century Baltimore, Scotch-Irish Presbyterian on one side, Quaker on the other. Once, late in life, Cass mused on the combined impact of his parents' Quaker and Puritan bloodlines, jesting, "What irks and rides me is a damnable sense of responsibility. It is an inheritance from my ancestors I think—Quakers—Puritans—Covenanters—Presbyterians, and Crusaders. What a lot they must have been." In fact, a good many of young Gilbert's more durable traits, including his adherence to the mythic Puritan injunction, "get behind thyself and push," sprang directly from the influence of his mother.

She hovered large in most of his scattered recollections of his Ohio childhood. One memory stands out among the rest. It centered on Zanesville's Presbyterian church: "In my boyhood, my brothers and myself attended church and Sunday School there with our mother, riding in from 'The Pines' on the Frazeyburg road in fair weather or foul, regarding our church attendance as the most important duty of the week." While organized religion would not loom overly large in Gilbert's adult life, all the Protestant cultural values associated with "going to church," which he absorbed as a boy, remained at the core of his character.[4]

In spring 1868 the mother gathered her sons and important family possessions, including a carriage, five horses, two parrots, and a monkey, journeyed to Marietta on the Ohio River, caught a packet boat downstream to Cairo, Illinois, and then headed up the Mississippi to join her husband in St. Paul. He died soon after their arrival.

Elizabeth Wheeler Gilbert, ca. 1890s.
(Photo by Steckel of Los Angeles, MHS Collections)

Mother and sons were left with Samuel's Civil War pension and some scattered real estate holdings in their new city. Elizabeth Gilbert promptly took control of the family's financial and social affairs, and gutted through. She would remain the dominating influence in the lives of her sons until her death three decades later.[5]

A mania for the profits of quick growth was sweeping the Midwest. Minnesota had entered the Union in 1858. A decade later it remained a raw postfrontier society. Ojibwe people kept up their seasonal rounds in northern Minnesota; small bands of Dakota still lived in southern parts of the state, after the disastrous U.S.–Dakota War of 1862. Closer to the cities freshly whitewashed Greek Revival farmhouses, and here and there a brick Italianate, were replacing the log huts of early wheat farmers. St. Paul was the biggest city in the state, growing fast, at the head of navigation on the Mississippi River. Thirty years before, it had been a cluster of ratty shacks called Pig's Eye, the nickname of the region's pioneering whiskey merchant. ("Westward the jug of Empire takes its way," Mark Twain quipped after listening to some local history during a visit in 1882.) By the early 1870s, as it filled with Irish, German, and American-born newcomers, St. Paul had become the banking and transportation center of the upper Northwest. The business of its tangled downtown streets generated the wealth that made Summit Avenue, running along a ridge above the city, the chosen site of its finest new homes. Fresh residential districts were being platted everywhere around. Just to the west, the even newer city of Minneapolis, the milling center of the region and increasingly Scandinavian in its ethnic mix, was beginning to outpace St. Paul's growth rate. This inspired an overheated boomers' rivalry between the two cities that would last well into the next century.[6]

Meanwhile, the Gilbert family, widow and sons, struggled in their new home, straitened but not flattened. The father had left them some downtown St. Paul commercial property, which yielded a modest rental income, and a small house on Aurora Avenue—located near the future site of the new state capitol, which Cass Gilbert would design twenty-seven years later. Cass's mother managed through the 1870s (as she would frequently remind her sons in later years) with no carriage, no horses, and only one servant. Under her watchful care, the sons completed the schooling they had begun back in Ohio. After that, Cass briefly attended a preparatory school in St. Paul, which later became Macalester College.[7]

Early on his mother noticed that Cass was different from his brothers—more talented, more artistic, more sensitive and vulnerable. "I do not wish to do injustice to the other boys," she wrote to him in a birthday greeting, "for their natures are different, and they have not as keen a sense of the higher duties and pleasures of life as you have." But she also wondered if he knew enough about coping with everyday realities on his own. "I worry about Cass," she told a friend somewhat protectively, "because he does not seem fitted to walk the ordinary paths of life."[8]

She needn't have worried. Even as a boy Cass was not the sort to hang back. He later remembered spending several happy teenage summers away from his mother's home, at work and play out in the countryside far from St. Paul. One summer in western Minnesota, while off horseback riding by himself on the prairie, he crossed paths with a traveling band of Dakota. Some young horsemen broke off to look him over and cantered alongside him ominously for a while until they finally pulled up and trotted off. Cass then galloped away as fast as he could. It was a scary experience at the time. Another summer he worked for a carpenter in the town of Red Wing on the Mississippi south of St. Paul, probably his first hands-on work in the craft of building.[9]

Then in September 1876, at age sixteen, Cass quit school to enter a draftsman's apprenticeship with architect Abraham Radcliffe, who had been pursuing a modest St. Paul practice since 1858. A boyhood chum named Clarence Johnston, who became Gilbert's closest friend, was already at work in Radcliffe's office. Little is known of their training under Radcliffe. They surely prized the practical skills they acquired, and happily exploited Radcliffe's office library, but later references to him in their correspondence suggest that their respect for his authority was not boundless. In fact, their shared reservations about Radcliffe's competence as a mentor fortified their good feelings toward one another. Gilbert and Johnston were headed toward an important rivalry in Minnesota architecture; however, these tensions still lay far ahead. For the moment their camaraderie was intimate and satisfying. Both were caught up in a craft that consumed their young enthusiasm. Each admired the ethic of headlong hard work he detected in the other. They were mesmerized by the new Boston-based national journal of architectural news and knowledge, *American Architect and Building News,* just beginning its long career in 1876. Their shared passion for the minutiae of their new calling combined with keen friendship to moderate for the moment the diverging momentum of their separate ambitions.[10]

Summer 1878 found Cass working in Wisconsin as a surveyor for the field engineer of the Hudson & River Falls Railroad. A letter home to Clarence (who was still working for Radcliffe in St. Paul) provides a quick glimpse into his social life that summer. His work crew was invited out one Saturday night by local contractors for some warm-weather refreshments. "First we had an ice cream," Cass reported, "then a lemonade on that, then cigars were brought out (which I refused), then more lemonade, more cream, more cigars, music by the band, and I retired to leave the contractors trying to get even with each other on the cigars-beer-cider-fruits &c 'ad nauseum.'" The prim undertone in this account was characteristic. Neither Cass's nor Clarence's pursuit of personal pleasure involved much carousing or self-indulgence. They were two serious and unusually ambitious youngsters hoping to make their mark in the world. By the end of that summer both were ready for a larger and more elevating architectural challenge than the Northwest could provide.[11]

2

Massachusetts Institute of Technology

In September 1878 Cass and Clarence set out by train for Boston to study architecture at the Massachusetts Institute of Technology, the preeminent center for architectural training in America. For the two young Minnesotans, the journey east was their chance to move from the edge of their chosen profession to its inner circle. The prospect was alluring.

On arrival in Boston, they settled together into rented rooms on Brookline Road, close by the swampy Back Bay Fens near the future site of Fenway Park, home of the Boston Red Sox. From their rooming house it was a long urban walk downtown to MIT. The entire institute was housed in Rogers Hall, an imposing neoclassical structure (built in 1866, destroyed in 1939) on the corner of Boylston and Berkeley Streets, just west of Boston's Public Garden. Their daily route to Rogers Hall took Cass and Clarence past Copley Square, where they could gaze at Trinity Church, the freshly finished granite masterpiece of Boston's most celebrated architect, Henry Hobson Richardson. Sketchbook in hand, Cass would visit Trinity repeatedly in the coming months. For the moment, though, the young men's main goal was to acquaint themselves with the architectural library and third-floor drafting rooms of Rogers Hall. They were eager to start work there under MIT's renowned architectural mentor, William Robert Ware.[1]

Professor Ware, scion of one of Boston's more prominent Unitarian families and a refined gentleman of Brahmin bearing, was much admired for his artistic and scholarly credentials, as well as for his social niche. He had graduated from Harvard College in 1852, studied further at Harvard's Lawrence Scientific School, and then apprenticed under blueblood Boston architect Edward Cabot. In 1859 he went to New York to train with Richard Morris Hunt, the first American graduate of the Ecole des Beaux-Arts in Paris. From Hunt, Ware learned to honor the Ecole as the fountainhead of architectural education in the Western world. After setting up his own practice in Boston, Ware joined in partnership with Henry van Brunt, another

William Robert Ware, ca. 1880s.
(MIT Museum)

product of Hunt's office, in 1864. A year later, dissatisfied with the scattershot training that most aspiring young American architects were receiving from office apprenticeships, Ware accepted an offer from MIT, then just getting underway, to organize its program for more systematic architectural instruction. The need for institutional training was urgent in his mind. In America, he told his new colleagues at the institute, "the art of building, upon which more money is spent, and more money misspent, than upon any other, is handed down from generation to generation by personal tradition alone." To remedy this, he promptly headed for Paris to look into the teaching methods of the Ecole. He intended to bring those methods back to Boston and install them at MIT.[2]

The life of the Ecole des Beaux-Arts spanned 150 years from 1819 to 1968, but its antecedents reached back to the architectural ambitions of Louis XIV, the seventeenth-century Sun King. The school's long domination of formal trans-Atlantic architectural expression lasted from Louis Napoleon's mid-nineteenth century Second Empire until World War I. Then, after several decades of wobbly retreat from the thrust of twentieth-century modernism, the Ecole came apart at the hands of Parisian student rebels in the radical insurgency of 1968. In retrospect, this final fate seems oddly appropriate. The nostalgic mood and educational mission of the Ecole would have abused the values of the academic Left almost anywhere in the world in the 1960s.[3]

The Ecole had brought system, depth, and competition, as well as a certain rigidity, to the tasks of architectural problem solving. Respectable success in mastering the intricate processes of structural design was the implicit goal of Beaux-Arts training. It demanded of its students a broad cultural background in history, the arts, and the mathematical sciences. Its expectations about the honing of refined skills in drawing and draftsmanship were stringent. It promoted an awareness of the subtleties of spatial planning in an urban context. It exalted the importance of beauty, often monumentally defined, sometimes to the neglect of functional utility. For the persevering student these priorities came into focus on a sequence of assigned design problems—a guild hall for example, a museum, enclosures for a palace garden, and so on. Perspective sketches for each project, followed by measured plans, sections, and elevations, were relentlessly evaluated by mentors and older students and reworked until they were finally judged to be acceptable. In rare cases they might even be found worthy of awards for excellence. The entire learning experience enforced a discipline of deference to one's seniors and to established codes and habits. While the Ecole was never exclusively committed to any particular architectural style, its insistence on mastery of the classical orders made it the historical center for the perpetuation of French Renaissance styling—known by the end of the nineteenth century simply as "Beaux-Arts."[4]

After two years in Europe, mainly studying the methods of the Ecole and its surrounding ateliers in Paris, Professor Ware launched his new architectural program at MIT in 1868. His four-year curriculum spanned a broad liberal arts spectrum, from history and foreign languages to math and chemistry. A special shorter course emphasized history, design, and drawing. In cobbling together both sequences, Ware made every effort to emulate the techniques and goals of the Ecole, though his Boston program clearly suffered from the outset by comparison with the crystallized reputation of the Parisian school and its students' ready access to Europe's architectural riches.

Boston was no Paris, but its architecture was beginning to take on a wide variety. Ware himself contributed to the mix through his ongoing partnership with Henry van Brunt. Both men's taste had been stretched from the prevailing Gothic Revival of the American 1850s by their introduction to contemporary French classicism under Richard Morris Hunt. Still, they nursed a lingering mistrust of the vernacular versions of Roman and Greek classicism, which had flourished in America in the early nineteenth century. It was a time when, in Ware's words, "all Christendom blossomed out with Doric banks, mints, and custom-houses; and we have to this day little pine Parthenons all over New England." Most of Ware and van Brunt's surviving post–Civil War collaborations—including First Church

(1867) on Marlborough Street in Boston, Harvard's grand Memorial Hall (1878) in Cambridge, and their buildings for the Episcopal Seminary (1871) off Brattle Street in Cambridge—rose outside the classical tradition, and reflected the contemporary popularity of the Gothic Picturesque, which was being promoted in the influential writings of the English critic John Ruskin.[5]

Although Ware's academic commitment to the classical tradition would harden soon, his main aim across the postwar years was not to enforce any single style but rather to enhance the general quality of architectural design in America, and the professional caliber of its practitioners. He asserted these goals not only in his management of the program at MIT but also in the crucial thrust he gave to the founding in 1876 of the new weekly journal, *American Architect and Building News*. The *AABN* was destined to dominate the American architectural conversation well into the twentieth century. "We are not going to fight the battle of the styles," an early issue assured its readers. Rather, under its young editor, Ware's nephew William Rotch Ware (freshly returned himself from study at the Ecole des Beaux-Arts), the journal's purpose, like that of the MIT program, was to foster a keener national awareness of architectural standards and possibilities. In fact, the *AABN* gave scope and vector to Cass Gilbert's and Clarence Johnston's teenage aspirations, and was crucial in their decision to head east for MIT in the fall of 1878.[6]

As it turned out, their time together in Boston was brief. Short on cash, neither lad quite knew how long he could stay at MIT. Both enrolled in Professor Ware's special two-year short course. Clarence, the more gregarious of the two, ran into money problems early on. Just four months into the academic year, he was forced to return home to St. Paul and take up apprentice work again. Cass's nest egg, for the coming year at least, was somewhat more secure, but he remained dependent on his widowed mother, who kept close control of the family's modest inheritance. She promised Cass twenty-five dollars a month for living expenses in Boston but made clear that this support would stop when he turned twenty-one, in another two years. So he plunged into his studies at the institute with a sense of living in the nick of time—driven by large dreams about his personal future, dreams he knew his mother shared.[7]

His time at MIT was not easy. He made his presence felt right away. A slender, well-buttoned young man with a quick tongue and assertive manner, he turned out to be a rather prickly fellow with whom to live. Concern for his social status at the institute as a fresh young upstart from the Midwest was one reason. His modest back-country origins, in sharp contrast to Boston's mannered East Coast insularity, fueled his need for attention and respect. Alone and anxious after Clarence's departure, he often found himself at odds with fellow students and even with his new mentors. Despite an occasional evening spent singing or portrait sketching in gatherings in other students' rooms, he reported to Clarence that he was homesick and "lonely as the deuce."[8]

His morale hardly improved when he failed after several tries to find a new roommate. The likeliest prospect was James Knox Taylor, also from St. Paul, a second-year student at the institute, whom Cass knew well from high school days. Good friends once, and destined to be very close colleagues in later years, Cass and Jim troubled each other during their year together at the institute. After Jim declined to live with him, Cass wrote him off as careless, frivolous, and disloyal. Taylor ran with a crowd, led by a self-assured young New Yorker named Arnold Brunner, that constantly disparaged Cass's work. Cass decided that Taylor lacked aesthetic sensibility and was probably "thinking of a fat position in a comfortable office rather than of artistic aspirations and delights." Only when the tension of the year at MIT was past would Cass cheerfully report that he and Jim were "now on the best of terms." Six years later, back in St. Paul, they would bond in architectural partnership.[9]

So it went with others. Cass made what turned out to be some durable friendships at MIT, but his spirited self-regard and competitive instincts ruffled his day-to-day personal relations in lecture halls and drafting rooms all year long. "I had to combat single-handed bigotry, jealousy, and fixed traditions," he told Clarence when it was over.

When Clarence proved the mettle of his own friendship for Cass by reprimanding his behavior from time to time, Cass took it well. "Your advice about my manner of speech is excellent," he replied on one occasion, "I say too much and mean too little. It is an old fault of mine and one not easily broken off. I think I have partially controlled my tongue lately and in time may outgrow the habit." Sorting through his other frailties, Cass also managed to acknowledge "that audacious egotism that is one of my amiable traits." The self-awareness in these phrases, edged with a trace of wit, reflected his growing psychological maturity. But he still had a long way to go.[10]

Professor Ware took his feisty new student from the Midwest in stride. A cultivated, graying bachelor with a fatherly manner, known among his students as "Billy Bobby," Ware left a strong impression on young Cass. Mainly he fixed in Cass beyond argument the bedrock conviction of the day that the cumulative flow of the long past should forecast the architectural future. Doubtless he was also influential in shaping the preference emerging in Cass for grounded practicality over free-floating abstract theory. But like the young Louis Sullivan, who had spent a year at the institute six years earlier, Cass found Ware's meticulous lectures in architectural history a shade tedious. (Ware was "not imaginative enough to be ardent," Sullivan recalled in his autobiography, adding that his introverted lecture style allowed him to ignore classroom spitball games while he moved through his "cemetery of orders and styles.") Reporting home to Clarence on the progress of Ware's history course, Cass said that the lectures on classical Greece were interesting enough but lacked originality. Clarence could read Rosengarten on "Greek" to get the gist of them.[11]

Albert Rosengarten was a German scholar whose massive book of 1857 on architectural styles appeared in English in 1876. The preface to the new edition described him as a "classical professor" who regarded ancient Greek and Roman originals as desirable models of taste for contemporary nineteenth-century architecture. It then noted that, since classical forms were beginning to influence American building fashion once again, Rosengarten's text provided an appropriate antidote to the recent celebration of the Gothic in the writings of the cultural sage John Ruskin, as well as the English architect Sir Gilbert Scott and the French theorist Viollet le Duc.[12]

Professor Ware was clearly coming to share Rosengarten's angle of vision. From the 1870s on, Ware's aesthetic preferences tilted ever more decisively toward the five orders of classical architecture, which he would one day lovingly detail in his own text, *The American Vignola* (1902). Of course not all of Ware's students fell into step with the classical resurgence. Most famously, Louis Sullivan did not. He remembered doubting what he had been taught at MIT about the classical orders representing "Platonic perfection." Another student of the 1870s wryly recalled that "for weeks we were upheaving and absorbing the whole Roman civilization, from Romulus all through the Caesars."[13]

Cass too had trouble with classicism. Reflecting on his year at MIT, he told Clarence: "My mind is cramped down to the narrow limits of style, correctness, usage and tradition rather than beauty, truth, and love of art . . . I am afraid now [that] I feel and think like my abomination, 'a classical architect.' Which of Ruskin's works shall I read as an antidote?" This last query is notable. Another dozen years would pass before Gilbert moved beyond the Ruskinian affection for the "picturesque" to accept the label "classical architect." He needed the neoclassical Chicago "White City" of 1893 to resolve his thoughts about the greatest stylistic rivalry of the nineteenth century. And even after that, for the rest of his life, he would practice an often startling stylistic versatility, spanning the range from Greek to Gothic, classical to picturesque, within the boundaries of the broad mainstream.[14]

He took great pleasure in architectural variety, which he indulged in his pencil and watercolor sketches. He was a talented freehand artist and turned often to his sketchbooks for recreational release. He carefully saved the best of his work and later enjoyed exhibiting examples from it. Dozens of his architectural sketches survive in scattered archives today. With rare exceptions, these sketches shun the classical for more picturesque forms and images. Throughout his career one can detect a recurring tension between the dominant architectural priorities of his office and clients on the one hand, and his personal artistic instincts on the other.

Gilbert's touchy nature during his year at MIT ensured that this tension between instinct and acquired training would flare with some frequency. It showed early on in relations with his MIT drawing teacher, Eugene Letang, an Ecole des Beaux-Arts graduate who joined Professor Ware as an assistant in 1871. Letang was a candid and effective mentor, looming warm and earnest in the recollections of men whose young talents he labored to improve. (Louis Sullivan remembered him as "sweaty" but "absorbed in teaching.") Letang effectively honed Gilbert's artistic knack. But Cass left clear evidence of the friction that could flash between them. Letang's bluntness in evaluating one of Gilbert's drawing problems, a billiard hall with belvedere, stung him. "I am thoroughly disgusted with Letang," Cass reported to Clarence. "I think there is no hope for him. He got very mad and we had an exceedingly lively talk." On a later occasion a critique of one of Gilbert's competition entries by Professor Ware himself dismayed the youngster. "I was most rakingly criticized by Mr. Ware," Cass told Clarence, adding that as a result his entry lost in the subsequent class vote. Cass in the classroom was quick but not serene, especially when his artist's eye and hand were at issue. He bruised easily but healed fast. "I am very proud of my architectural drawings," he soon reported, "and I can safely say that there was not another portfolio in the [institute] that could surpass mine."[15]

His happiest hours in Boston were away from his critics, when he filled his sketchbook with his eye and instincts. This of course was not mere recreation. An article of faith in the Beaux-Arts teaching of Letang and Ware was the functional value of drawing and redrawing to clarify one's command of style and structure. What is significant is that all the buildings Cass sketched that year stood notably outside the classical canon. They included several Ware and van Brunt buildings in Boston, Cambridge, and nearby Worcester; a rail station and insurance block by the Boston firm of Peabody and Stearns; a polychromatic suburban residence in Milton by William Ralph Emerson;

a Richard Upjohn Gothic church in Norwich, Connecticut; and Richardson's two great Boston churches, the Brattle Square Church on Commonwealth Avenue and Trinity nearby on Copley Square. Cass was so pleased with his sketch of Trinity's cloister that he showed it on visits to architectural offices in Boston—another pastime he greatly enjoyed.[16]

Trinity Church, Boston, H. H. Richardson, 1872–77.
(Photo by author)

Perhaps his climactic thrill that year was a chance encounter with Richardson himself. Gilbert described it this way twenty-five years later:

> I remember one day descending the interminable stairway from the attic of the old Rogers Hall and about half way down encountered a man of swarthy complexion and huge proportions mount-

H. H. Richardson dressed as a monk.

(Photo by George Collins Cox, 1883, courtesy of the Society for the Preservation of New England Antiquities.)

> ing the stairs. I remember an impression of a flaming note of color in a large red and yellow necktie that looked as though it were trying to escape from his waistcoat and set fire to the building. He was a man of such extraordinary appearance that my attention was arrested at once and I wondered what he could possibly want in the building. As we passed he stopped me and with a singularly charming voice and manner asked some simple question and I guided him to Professor Ware who occupied a little room in the building adjacent to the library where I learned that my companion was the then already famous Henry Hobson Richardson.

Gilbert went on to recall that several years later he visited Richardson at his home in suburban Brookline:

> Here he presided like a medieval potentate over a group of devoted adherants [*sic*]. Everything about him was large, generous and impressive. His library, where he received me, was a room of unusual dimensions, on one side was a huge fireplace and in the middle an enormous table covered with architectural books of large dimensions. Richardson was a man of big mind and big figure; everything about him was big, but with it all his manner was so genial and kindly and delightful that one involuntarily yielded to his infectious enthusiasms. He was one of the greatest personalities that I remember to have met. Few men have left such an impression upon their day and generation.

Parts of these recollections read as if the middle-aged Gilbert were reciting a legend. Clearly for the nineteen-year-old who met the master on the staircase of Rogers Hall in the winter of 1879 it was a moment to cherish. The remembered encounter dramatized for Cass a special aesthetic debt. Richardson's hand would influence Gilbert's architecture profoundly after his return to St. Paul and for years to come.[17]

His year at the institute ended on another high note, alive with personal satisfaction. In late winter 1879, despite a siege of bad health brought on by long hours, limited sleep, and no gymnasium exercise, he decided to drive for a place of academic honor in his class, throwing his competitive energies into the final sequence of architectural problems presented by Professor Ware. One of them, a "Pompeian

Restoration," took Cass to the Boston Athenaeum on Beacon Street for a week of earnest research on ancient Pompeii. "I have denied myself everything to work," he told Clarence. "I have given over all pleasure, all society, all amusements to carry out my one idea of work, and hard work." He turned work into a moral contest: "I have learned to combat for the right, I have learned to overcome opposition by quiet perseverance, and this is more than I ever knew before."

Three prominent members of the Boston chapter of the American Institute of Architects judged the class's work to determine the chapter's annual awards. In a letter to Clarence, Cass shouted the result: "Hurrah I have the 2nd Prize." First prize went to Jim Taylor's friend Arnold Brunner, an adversary all year long. But nothing could diminish Cass's sense of victory. The enduring psychological value of the prize showed in the way he magnified it later on. "I hold no degree from any University or College," he told the president of the University of Texas, an important potential client, in 1910, "although curiously enough I received the prize of my class at the Institute of Technology over thirty years ago at a time when degrees were not granted within the special architecture course." In the afternoon of his career, colleagues would lavish Cass with prizes. None meant more to him than the one that ended his lonely year at MIT.[18]

In fact one year at the institute was enough for Cass. Even as he left for a badly needed vacation on the island of Nantucket off Cape Cod, he was laying ambitious plans to spend his next year in Europe. He proposed to Clarence that they sail together for England and then the continent, to study and sketch the great architecture of the Western world at its sources. Money was a problem for both of them, but Cass believed that apprenticeships in the offices of London architects would finance their travel. A good mix of European jobs and journeys was surely preferable to another year at MIT. Cass had even selected and listed his London architects: George Edmund Street, Norman Shaw, Albert Waterhouse, William Burges. Significantly, most of them worked within the English Gothic Revival tradition, which Cass associated with the critic John Ruskin and the architect Sir Gilbert Scott. Cass enormously admired Scott's work and regretted his recent death. But Scott had helped train Street, and Street had helped train Shaw, and Cass thought of his whole list as an architectural school he wanted to join. Beyond that, the idea of working under a prominent architect and absorbing some of his glory, he confessed to Clarence, was a powerful attraction.[19]

Clarence disappointed Cass by deciding not to join him on the European journey. Cass resolutely set about rounding up money to carry out the venture by himself. His mother's monthly allotment, plus funds from generous relatives in Zanesville and savings from a summer job, would see him through. The summer job came from one of his father's old friends, who invited Cass to join a surveying party for the Coast and Geodetic Survey, working along the Hudson River Highlands near West Point. Cass found the work tiresome, but it gave him plenty of spare time for architectural sketching. The number of attractive buildings along the Hudson seemed rather meager, however. "How can I sketch architecture when there is none to sketch?" he asked Clarence rhetorically. "How am I to think and form when the sunset is my only example of color and the rocks and trees the only beautiful forms? . . . How eagerly I have looked at building after building, in vain hopes of something to stay my appetite. . . ." But the appetite persisted: "I sketch, I draw, I scrawl, I seldom think. My ideas become dulled from lack of use."

He ended this restless lament on a more cheerful note. There was a detail of Gothic architecture he had yet to master: "The subject of finials, you know, was always one on which I stranded high and dry. I took to sketching . . . all the finials I could think of, so as to have a stock in case of sudden necessity." Here he paused to sketch into his letter a dozen different Gothic finials, so that Clarence in St. Paul could share his supply.

Cass was clearly ready for Europe.[20]

3

Europe

Gilbert spent the fall of 1879 getting ready for his European journey—the first of some two-dozen overseas excursions he would embark upon during his lifetime. Europe was the essential next step in his architectural education. The venture would connect him to a cultural tradition of high importance in the history of American travel—overseas tourism.

By the late nineteenth century, American tourism abroad had become a cherished experience, though it lured as yet a much smaller crowd than it would over the next century. In the 1870s Baedeker guides and their competitors, already revised through several editions, spoke to a select audience of cultivated ladies and gentlemen whose overseas journeys set them apart from the ordinary American. What distinguished these people was that they shared an implicit belief in the relative superiority of European history, art, literature, music, and architecture over American examples. This grounded them in a profoundly colonial sense of American culture. But the belief served vital social needs among them. It allowed them to share the experience of Europe, as well as a collective pride in that experience, with one another after they came home. Thus the "Grand Tour." That phrase sprang up as early as the 1670s to describe what polite English parents came to think of as the capstone of their children's education and an embellishment of their own—a carefully planned reconnaissance of the European continent. By the 1820s a few Americans were joining the tour, and by the 1870s their presence in growing numbers had become part of its ambience. Novelist Henry James described them as "those representatives of our race . . . curious of foreign opportunity and addicted to foreign sojourns." They were the New World's earliest genteel tourists.[1]

A venture into Europe by a solitary young American like Cass Gilbert aspiring to the status of a gentleman required special social connections. This meant a stack of letters of introduction from fellow Americans who were prepared to vouch for him to those Europeans willing to receive him. In the Gilded Age, social interaction with important strangers depended heavily on such letters. In the American party politics of the age, these connections were called one's "Influence." Marshalling this influence was the way to secure a government job under the prevailing spoils system. Beyond the political arena, in the cultivated private lives of ladies and gentlemen who did not know each other, the quiet display of one's credentials—one's network of social influence—was an expected propriety.

Gilbert gathered as many letters as he could—from Professor Ware and other architects in Boston—designed to ease his entry into the offices of architects in London and elsewhere. He secured letters from old friends of his father to technical and scientific colleagues in Europe, and from elected Minnesota politicians to assure good treatment at American consulates and legation offices overseas. All this was normal. It was the way one traveled through the tiers of social status at home and abroad. Violation of the rules was a social mistake, subtle but instantly noted. Cass was a quick study in this behavioral art and a skilled practitioner for the rest of his life. His ultimate mastery of the intricacies of status politics would make him seem to friends sometimes a bit punctilious. Already at age nineteen he was learning fast.

He worried about landing in England as an American alone among Englishmen but assured himself that the English, after all, "at the very best are only our equals." Their renowned rebuffs of strangers, he believed, need not bruise his "national dignity." He hoped whenever possible to tap into the universal brotherhood that he felt joined artists everywhere in a special calling that set them apart from the crowd. He wanted to belong to that fraternity. He vowed that among his new acquaintances, "I will not be to them an American but an artist." Promoting the social status of the artist would continue to rank among his most dogged lifetime projects.[2]

Just before leaving for Europe he joined a bittersweet family reunion in Zanesville, where a cousin whose wedding he had attended the year before was dying of tuberculosis. On the way to Ohio from Boston, Cass recorded a reverent glimpse from his train window of the unfinished new state capitol in Albany, New York. Construction of this building, originally designed by Canadian architect Thomas Fuller, began in 1867 but soon fell into scandalous controversy over cost and taste. H. H. Richardson was now collaborating with fellow architect Leopold Eidlitz and landscape designer Frederick Law Olmsted to revise and complete the building—perhaps the most widely

South façade, New York State Capitol, Albany, H. H. Richardson (with Leopold Eidlitz), 1876–83.
(Photo by author)

publicized architectural reform project of the 1870s. Cass had hoped to stop and tour the Albany capitol, but gazing at it from a moving train at a distance had to suffice. His admiration for Richardson remained boundless. In fact if job hunting in London should fail, he told friend Clarence, he planned to head back to Boston to seek a place in the master's office.[3]

In Zanesville he joined his mother, who had come down from St. Paul for the family crisis. After the death and burial of his cousin, he left with his mother for Washington to gather still more letters of introduction for his European journey. Then on the morning of January 3, 1880, his version of the Grand Tour finally got underway as he headed for the Cunard Piers in lower Manhattan to board the steamer *Scythia*. After waving goodbye to his mother and to James Knox Taylor, who to his pleasant surprise showed up to see him off, he went directly to his stateroom and swallowed a dose of potassium bromide. It did no good. He was fearfully seasick for the next twelve days. Reaching Liverpool was a great relief. He mused that when the time came he might avoid the Atlantic crossing by going home through Siberia and Alaska.[4]

Upon arrival in England he was struck with what American visitors for centuries have felt it urgent to report on first impression—the mistiness of English skies and her often fogbound towns and cities. On the way from Liverpool to London the cathedral at Lichfield and school buildings of Rugby were pale silhouettes, and the foggy obscurity of London itself was beyond anything he had known before. At times he could not see across the street. London air, never very salubrious, was dirtier than ever before or since, owing to the sprawling coal-fueled furnace workshops of that era. Cass did not like the city at all on first acquaintance. Its foul air, heavy with gas and coal smoke, left him red-eyed and constantly sneezing. When a stranger surprised him by asking if he were an Italian, he looked in a mirror and found "the London fog so ground in that my complexion was that of a dirty organ-grinder." Moreover London's most famous buildings, Gothic and classical alike, disappointed him. He found Westminster Abbey very dark and dingy, and its nave looked "gaunt" and "hungry" to him. Sir Christopher Wren's St. Paul's Cathedral owed its grandeur to its size alone, he decided. As for the rest of Wren's late seventeenth-century Renaissance work in London, his judgment was firm: "I haven't the slightest admiration for it." (In later years, after his decisive conversion from Ruskin's Gothic passions to Renaissance classicism, Wren's buildings became venerated icons for Gilbert, and he would label Wren "the consummate Master of his time.")[5]

What did win his eye in London were its many modern shop fronts. They were different from what he was used to seeing at home. In America in the 1870s, designers of tall new urban commercial structures often layered their vertical dimension with heavy surface complexities to distract viewers and users from the embarrassment of abnormal height. What Cass noticed in the London store buildings was a striking visual uniformity rising from the big show windows at street level. He sketched an example for Clarence. "The beauty of it

Dome, St. Paul's Cathedral, London, Sir Christopher Wren, ca. 1675–1710. (Photo by author)

was its simple arrangement of forms. The mouldings were very flat and the carving was clear and sharp," he wrote. "But the main thing I wanted to speak of was the repetition of design in the [upper] stories of the building. . . . The simplicity of the design was a lesson to me." The lesson sank in. Gilbert would put it to work a decade later when he joined other urban architects in puzzling through the aesthetic problem of the tall building.[6]

Before leaving for the continent, he made a side trip to Southampton, which included long pauses at Salisbury Cathedral and the old market town of Romsey on the River Test. Romsey's fine twelfth-century Norman abbey church, warmed by soft sunlight filtering through the mist, impressed him, and the placid atmosphere surrounding it prompted a perceptive observation about the difference between England and America: Romsey was "ancient, picturesque, and English to the last degree; quaint is no name for such places. We would not tolerate them in America, we love them in England." This last comment spoke to the habit common among American boomers—then as now—of scrapping their physical past to make way for commercial growth. It also suggests that Cass was more ready than he had been in Boston to join the counter trend—the new affection for all things "early" and "colonial" just beginning to spread among American East Coast architects.[7]

After his two weeks in England, Paris captivated Cass, and he stayed there longer than he had planned. Veteran tourists testified that the Paris of 1880 lacked some of the confident charm that had radiated from Louis Napoleon's proud Second Empire before the brief terror of the 1871 Paris Commune. For young Cass, however, Paris was unspoiled excitement. From his room in the Latin Quarter near the Ecole des Beaux-Arts, he joined a throng of young Americans clustered there, some of them students at the Ecole, most not. He happily toured the school and swapped gossip about it, while trying to improve his fractured French. He wished he could stay and join the Ecole. Meanwhile, he savored the easy egalitarianism of the Latin Quarter: "Every man is what his work makes him, and it is only an utter boor that is not received with open arms." The gregarious mood of cafe intercourse beguiled him. He began taking claret with his meals. "Everybody here drinks wine," he explained carefully to his dry mother in St. Paul. Other Parisian differences startled him. One was the presence in the streets of so many government officials, military and civilian, dressed in lavish ornamental uniforms. Another was the way everyone, officials and ordinary citizens alike, ignored ragged homeless men sprawling in the gutters. America was as yet still far from being that callous.[8]

Despite the chilly weather, Cass wandered with his sketchbook all over the city, thrilled by its architectural treasures. The Cathedral of Notre Dame left him awestruck—"of all the things I have ever seen, the most truly grand, noble and inspiring." And after Notre Dame, other long-awaited spectacles: the Louvre, the ruined sixteenth-century walls of the Tuilleries (burned by Communards in 1871), the grand vista of the Champs Elysées, Napoleon's Arc de Triomphe. On they came, an aesthetic and historical overload. Cass would nurse a lifelong consciousness that, unlike so many prominent architects of his generation, he never lived very long in Paris and never studied at the Ecole. Frequent visits had to do. He would come back to the city and its riches every chance he got.[9]

After Paris, for three months into the spring of 1880 Cass moved mainly by rail across the south of France through Italy and its seductive cities—Milan, Venice, Florence, Rome, Siena, Pisa, Genoa. Vivid images along the way filled his letters home. The "barbaric luxurience" of the Milan Cathedral. The interior of St. Mark's in Venice (more brilliant than Richardson's Trinity, he decided) where loose mosaic squares fell from the ceiling and clattered around him while he sketched. The stupendous marble and silver bathroom of the Medicis, with its tub of carved Carrara marble, in the Pitti Palace in Florence. The campanile of Florence's Palazzo Vecchio and the Baths of Diocletian in Rome, both inspiring quick watercolors. The Queen of Italy in procession on a crowded Roman street, looking right at Cass three feet away. ("She is one of the handsomest women I have ever seen and has such a good look," he told his mother. "I declare if she wasn't married I'd marry her myself, that is if you were willing.") The emerging ruins of the Roman Forum. The Colosseum by moonlight, which moved him to take off his hat in the night. The ball of St. Peter's atop its dome, where he climbed to gaze at the Mediterranean and "half of Italy." The dazzling white marble Gothic cathedral at Orvieto, a mountaintop Etruscan town of strong simple architecture mellow in the sunlight ("just the place we imagine when we think of Utopia and Arcadia"). The interior of the cathedral at Siena, even more compelling than Orvieto's, and Siena's decorative iron work, the best he had ever seen. Pisa's leaning tower, "not without some beauty."[10]

Cass was a contented tourist, and he managed some occasional self-mockery at being one. While entering the Uffizzi Gallery in Florence, he confessed, he asked if any of the Uffizzi family were still alive, only to learn that "Uffizzi" meant "office-holders." Crossing the Arno on the Ponte Vecchio in Florence, he found the shops along the bridge waiting for gullible Americans. He described to his mother what he saw for sale: "an ancient engraving of Penn's treaty with the Indians by Michel Angelo. Also the signing of the Declaration of In-

Colosseum, Rome.
(Photo by author)

Orvieto Cathedral, Arnolfo di Cambio, 1290–1500.
(Photo by author)

dependence by the same author. A sketch for a Centennial exposition building by Giotto, and several competitive designs by Raphael for the decoration of the interior of the Washington Monument." These cheap souvenirs and their naïve purchasers stirred in him the familiar genteel tourist's urge to distance himself from his fellow Americans.[11]

By mid-March 1880 he was ready for the most adventurous part of his tour—a springtime journey, mainly by foot, northward across central France, where trains were scarce and villagers unpredictable. From Lyon in the valley of the Rhone, where he paused to sketch some wrought-iron hinges on the doors of an ancient church, he set out for Blois through isolated small towns along winding country roads. Each day's hike brought a fresh sense of discovery and personal freedom. He had worried a bit before leaving America about the test of traveling alone on the continent. Now he found himself enjoying it hugely most of the time. One of his more graphic descriptions, in a letter home to Clarence, described his journey across the French countryside. It was as if he were living at last a cherished boyhood dream. "My costume is unique and quite serviceable not to say artistic," he wrote, a soft gray English hat with visors front and back, a rough brown jacket and matching pants, tan canvas leggings to protect the pants from the dirt of the road, guidebook, sketchbooks and sketching stool bound together with a leather strap, and a satchel slung over the shoulder, filled with watercolors, brushes and pencils, quinine, a flask of brandy, a pistol, and a change of underwear. To complete the description, he added a sketch of himself and his outfit. Tall, lean, and erect, sporting a flaring new mustache, he felt carefree, almost bohemian, out among the flowering fields and unknown villages. Even with the pleasant hours spent on his sketching stool he claimed to cover twelve to twenty miles a day meandering toward Normandy. France in the springtime turned him into a happy vagabond.[12]

When challenges came, he met them with some bravado. In the tiny town of Verierre in the upper valley of the Loire, a crowd gathered to watch him sketch. One villager, overly officious and aggressive, shoved his way forward and demanded to know who he was. Cass felt threatened. The rural patois of the region confused the confrontation. The urban French he had picked up in Paris cafes was no help. He finally pulled out his pistol in self-defense, whereupon the man pulled out his badge. He was the town mayor, and he demanded to see Cass's passport. Lacking a passport, Cass presented his letters of introduction, promoting one of them as a statement from the chief of the U.S. Department of War. When that didn't work, he flashed an envelope from his mother covered with official-looking stamps and addresses, calling it his passport. This finally seemed to satisfy the mayor. Cass packed his pistol, gathered his sketching tools, and hus-

"'Our special artist' veiwing [sic] *the promised land." Gilbert's sketch of himself, 1880.*
(From Clarence H. Johnston papers, MHS Collections)

tled out of town. Ten days later, in the town of Moulins, he ran out of money and had trouble using his letter of credit. To add weight to his identity he told the local banker that he had recently received First Prize in Architecture at the Institute of Technology in America. (It just came out that way, he told his mother. He did not mean to tell a lie.)[13]

Cass found Moulins, like other small towns along his route—Ambert, Clermont, St. Pourcain, Chambord, Blois—as rich in history as in architecture. The romance he savored from the French past, full of fortress sieges, battered chateaux, and captured kings, made the architecture glow more brightly for him. As his journey progressed he worked up a vast admiration for the buildings of the early sixteenth century, the age of Francois I. Even though he found the roof of the king's chateau at Chambord "as disordered as a maniac's brain," he liked the style immensely. He warned his mother that when he returned to practice in Minnesota she could expect to see his stylistic taste running to "old Chateaux and Flamboyant Cathedrals."

Chateau Chambord, Loire, France.
(Photo by Norman Craig)

The region around Chambord and Blois reminded him of Minnesota, he said, even though the Minnesota prairie lacked as yet an adequate array of ruined Gothic spires or castellated fortress walls.[14]

In a more sober mood, Cass recited for his mother the European architectural styles he had examined so far. The list read like a schoolboy's report: classic, Byzantine, Romanesque, Norman, English Gothic, French decorated Gothic, Venetian Gothic, flamboyant, Renaissance—each style followed by the names of places where Cass had seen and sketched the finest examples. In 1880 this was architectural field training at its best. As he returned to Paris for some final weeks in the Latin Quarter, he decided that his journey through Italy and central France had been "one of the great epochs in my life, and probably the most useful three months I will ever have put in."[15]

After so many weeks on the road alone, reuniting with his Parisian friends was important, too. "I dine at my old cafe," he wrote, "and meet there a crowd of the younger stars of American art such as gather no where else." The ideas and anecdotes, the brisk exchanges and friendly tabletop criticism charmed and warmed him. He discovered for the first time in his life the pleasures of male group companionship free from the stress of enforced competition. Also pleasant was the praise his architectural sketches won from his new companions, inspiring invitations to join in sketching jaunts around Paris and into the old towns of Belgium. Their encouragement quickened his impulse to excel in artistry and to understand better the nuances of blending painting, sculpture, and architecture. He didn't want Paris to end. "The time will come soon enough," he mused, "when I will work and lack praise, when I will do my best for others [who] will not appreciate my work, when the cares and hard work of business will destroy these dreams of idealism and this association with artists; why may I not now enjoy what is probably the golden period of my life. . . ." The prospect of leaving the cafes of Paris stirred in him an early sense of distance between the buoyant life of the carefree artist, for which a part of him yearned, and the future for which his family background and professional ambition prepared him. His thoughts anticipated what would turn out to be a durable tension structuring the young architect's career: the rivalry between designing buildings for aesthetic satisfaction and designing buildings to make money from people who wanted to use them. The tension was built into his chosen craft, and Cass would never escape it.[16]

Late in June 1880, after outings to Versailles and Chartres, and five days in Rouen that enraptured him—"the most wonderful town in all Europe for architecture"—Cass reluctantly left the continent. His return to England that summer flattened both his purse and his pride. Efforts to find an apprenticeship in a London architectural office failed miserably. None of his carefully gathered connections worked. In retrospect the reasons are clear. He had not reckoned with the current plight of the English construction industry. A nationwide economic slump had set in during the mid-1870s, bottomed out in 1879, and stayed low through the 1880s. So many people fell out of work that a new noun, the *unemployed*, entered the *Oxford English Dictionary* in 1882. Also the cluster of prominent English architects Cass had identified a year earlier as most worth working for was in momentary disarray following the death of Sir Gilbert Scott. William Burges and George Edmund Street, whose offices he visited, were both nearing death themselves. Norman Shaw, who would pursue his important career well into the twentieth century, was seriously ill in 1880. Alfred Waterhouse turned him down by mail before Cass could even make a call. He was told that with so many English draftsmen out of work it was unreasonable for an American stranger to expect prompt employment. Try as he might, he just could not land the sort of job he wanted to round out his trip and poise him to begin his practice.

The situation hurt and puzzled him: "No one seems to want me, yet all praise my work." By mid-July he was ready to give up. "I am clean discouraged," he now confessed to Clarence, "there is no use. I cannot find work here in London, and I am fast running out of money too." All he could do was come back to America, a full year sooner than he had planned. His mother mailed him the money. Summer's end found him in New York, looking for a job. His first Grand Tour ended in anticlimax. For all his disappointment about its lame conclusion, he counted on there being many more. Optimism about his longer future remained unspoiled.[17]

4

McKim, Mead and White

Cass had dreamed of joining H. H. Richardson's office in suburban Boston after his return from Europe. Instead he found himself reuniting with Clarence Johnston in New York City. Clarence, still his closest friend, had come east from St. Paul and landed a position in the office of Christian Herter, Manhattan's most stylish interior designer, who was hiring new assistants in summer 1880. Joining Johnston was Frank Bacon, who left the freshly organized New York firm of McKim, Mead and White for a new job at Herter's. Gilbert pounced for the place left open by Bacon's move. Here was his chance to enter the office soon to be hailed as the most influential architectural firm in America.

The opening at McKim, Mead and White brought Gilbert to Stanford White, who, at age twenty-six, was the firm's youngest partner. White already dominated the office mood. He was a tall, strapping fellow with a great shock of stiff red hair, compulsively energetic, theatrical in his living habits to the point of melodrama, and a brilliant architectural designer. He needed a new personal assistant. After several tries, Cass gained an interview with him, which he never tired of recalling. He arrived with a batch of his favorite European sketches. White shuffled through them, grabbed one, leaped up, and hurried next door to show it to senior partner William Mead, who managed the business of the firm. Mead was taken on the spot by Gilbert's artistry and White's enthusiasm. He offered Cass the job at twenty dollars a week, good pay in those days. Elated, Cass promptly went to work in a small alcove just off the firm's main drafting room at 57 Broadway—in later years a legendary address in the profession, crowded thick with young architects, sculptors, and muralists, working, drinking, and talking their way toward the promise of their futures.[1]

Mead, White, and Charles McKim had launched their partnership the year before, in 1879. White and McKim earlier served apprenticeships with Richardson. White had designed arresting interior details for several of Richardson's more celebrated spaces, including Trinity Church in Boston, the Senate Chamber in the New York State Capitol at Albany, and the library of the Watts Sherman House in Newport, Rhode Island. McKim, more reserved, more scholarly, more diplomatic, a veteran of the Ecole des Beaux-Arts, could not match White's flair for design but brought quality control and a broad professional outreach to the firm. Mead, who also carried the

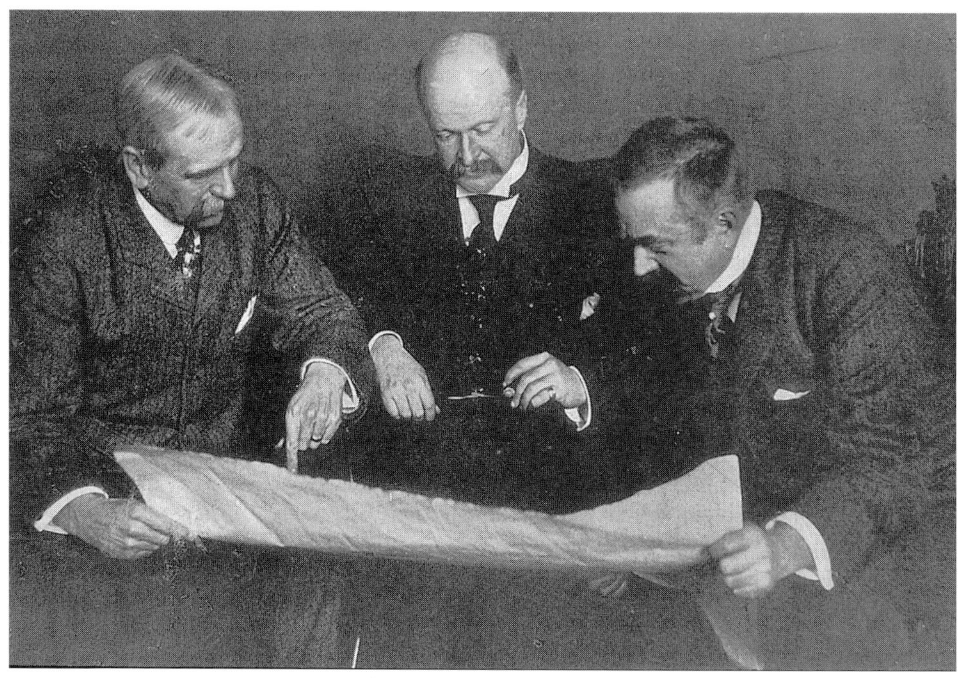

Charles McKim, William Mead, and Stanford White, ca. 1905.
(Avery Architectural and Fine Arts Library, Columbia University in the City of New York)

credentials of formal European training, was the firm's main planner. His office management helped temper the often volatile atmosphere at 57 Broadway. The three principals got on remarkably well most of the time, and their expanding staff of aides and draftsmen, Gilbert included, came to believe they were working with the best. "I feel as though I were in an atelier," one of them said. "It is not work, it is happiness to be here . . . and every day brings something new and good."[2]

The young men at 57 Broadway had the good luck to believe that they were nudging the American architectural profession toward a superior future. Many were convinced that something "new" and "modern" and "correct" was about to breeze through the feckless muddling of the current scene. Certainly the shoptalk of the early 1880s, at 57 Broadway and elsewhere, registered this attitude. Chicago architect John Wellborn Root sardonically commented about the judgmental agility of his colleagues: "With what thin disguise of recently acquired saintliness do we protest that a thing is bad to-day which yesterday we ceased doing and to-morrow will do again!"[3]

The young architects' yen for something new and better was authentic enough. Although the familiar phrases later used to describe American architectural taste during the decade after Appomattox—"reign of terror," "General Grant Gothic," "varnished barbarism," "Gilded Age"—did not catch on until a bit more distance had opened on the early postwar years, thoughts were clearly converging to enforce the dismissive scorn behind these phrases.

The postwar scene could be daunting to those interested in improving architectural expression. Even the finest monuments of the prewar Gothic revival—the sumptuous suburban villas of Alexander Jackson Davis, the castellated creations of James Renwick, the chaste elegance of Richard Upjohn's churches large and small—suffered in the shadow of the heavy "Victorian" ornament now being layered onto postwar versions of the Gothic. The writings of critics sympathetic to the Gothic mood—John Ruskin and his American disciples

Charles Eliot Norton and Russell Sturgis—retained continuing respect, but the quality of Gothic production in the United States seemed to many young practitioners to have been bastardized by the gross desires of its ever more prosperous post–Civil War clients.

Lyndhurst, Tarrytown, New York, Alexander Jackson Davis, 1838.
(Lyndhurst, a National Trust Historic Site)

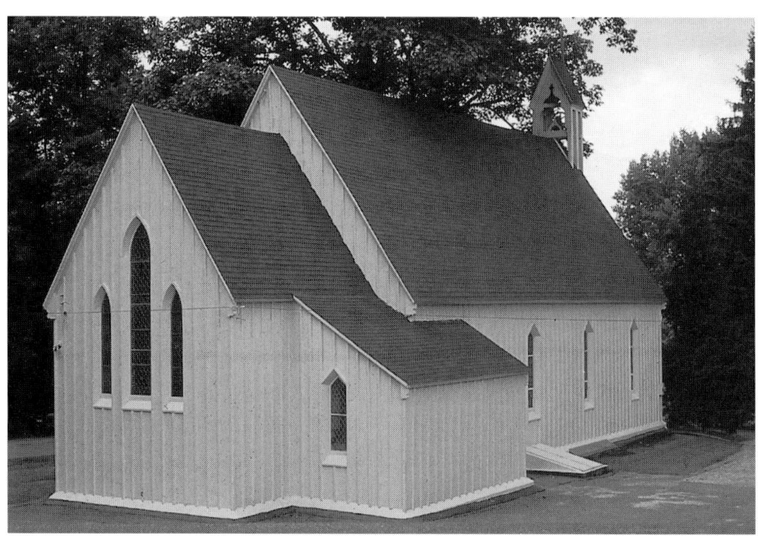

St. John's in the Wilderness Episcopal church, Copake Falls, New York, Richard Upjohn, 1850.
(Photo by author)

One of the young draftsmen at 57 Broadway later remembered the new buildings of the early '70s as "the ugliest structures ever raised by the labor of man." Another Gilbert contemporary, referring to the architectural taste of the *nouveaux riches* in postwar America, recalled, "The art of pretentiousness was never better understood, and no art has responded more quickly to a popular demand." Critiques of this sort applied not only to Victorian elaborations of the Gothic but also to urban mansions with mansard helmets of Second Empire vintage. Rich Americans lusting for the highest current fashion grabbed these imperious mansard mansions, much as they did lavish gowns from the Parisian House of Worth.[4]

Montgomery Schuyler and Mariana van Rensselaer, two architectural critics on the rise in the established journals of the day, pressed the indictment against postwar taste. Schuyler, in a lecture at Union College in Schenectady, condemned the "crudity" and "extravagance" of the "architectural freaks" erected in the early 1870s. In the *Century Magazine* series "Recent Architecture in America," van Rensselaer regretted the urge to "startle" that she discerned in the

Mansard style, Vermont state office building, Montpelier, ca. 1870.
(Photo by author)

complex angularity and over-adornment of contemporary architecture. "It is this desire," she wrote, "which has covered many buildings . . . with profuse, mistaken, disturbing decoration. It is this which has so corrupted our taste that we cannot appreciate simplicity, straightforwardness, common sense, and quiet beauty." Van Rensselaer found these latter charms embedded in the buildings of her favorite American architect, H. H. Richardson. She acknowledged, however, that his design preferences were so personal and idiosyncratic that they defied successful emulation. "Mr. Richardson's talent is of a very peculiar sort," she wrote. "Its results are, perhaps, a law unto themselves; but they are sometimes the last results in the world which should be made a law for others, or which could be safely diluted with the water of imitation. Take away the exuberant strength and fervor which enable Mr. Richardson at times to do unlawful things in a magnificently seductive way, and we should merely have the unlawfulness without the compensating charm."

While Richardson was the first American architect to have a style named after him—"Richardsonian Romanesque"—the boundaries of its appeal among clients and critics tended to coincide with the mystique of the master himself. After his untimely death at age forty-six, commentators would soon refer back to "the Richardsonian Interlude." But the impact of his genius on many young practitioners, including Cass Gilbert, lasted much longer than his vogue.[5]

The Philadelphia Centennial Exposition of 1876, coming toward the end of a long slump in building construction after the panic of 1873, infused young architects with a verve that helped overcome their glum reaction to the postwar situation. Many of the exposition's design models—especially the exhibition buildings of the several American states—were outdated and overwrought, but other models from foreign sources—English, Swiss, Japanese—stimulated fresh ideas.

"Queen Anne" was the name of the new English style introduced in Philadelphia. Its overstuffed American version, bulging with multiple bays, gables, porches, and lavish filigree, soon replaced the mansard as the new popular craze of the era. It spread like a virus. A few years later *American Architect and Building News* referred in passing to a client "who took the Queen Anne infection at an early stage of the epidemic." In a travelogue of 1886 Charles Dudley Warner pursued this theme: "That's the way with some towns. Queen Anne seems to strike them all of a sudden, and become epidemic. The only way to prevent it is to vaccinate, so to speak, with two or three houses, and wait; then it is not so likely to spread." But at the outset of its vogue Queen Anne intrigued many thoughtful Americans because it seemed to spring from English national roots. Its arrival for the centennial stimulated the novel notion that early *American* architecture might also hold stylistic promise for the Americans of 1876. Moreover, the state buildings that Massachusetts and Connecticut erected for the exposition were said to be "colonial" in style. Three versions of an American log cabin also appeared, the one from Mississippi covered with authentic dangling Spanish moss. Thus the centennial celebration helped to nurture not only the rush of Queen Anne but also a so-called colonial revival, reaching back to a home-grown American architectural deposit never widely valued before. This revival coincided with the sudden publication of hundreds of county histories inspired by the centennial. Together these enthusiasms reflected a nostalgic new fascination among urbanizing Americans for the simpler and more intimate aspects of their own rural past.[6]

In the summer following the centennial, McKim, Mead and White joined an unprecedented bent among American architects by veering off the beaten trails of normal summer travel to look over their own colonial architecture. They concentrated on the Atlantic seaboard towns north of Boston—Marblehead, Salem, Newburyport, and Portsmouth. Mead later recalled the trip as a turning point in their stylistic preferences. Though McKim had already developed an interest in the trim and precisely centered eighteenth-century Georgian architecture that abounded in these coastal towns, attention concentrated on an earlier and altogether different vein in the colonial deposit—the more rambling and cumulative shingle-clad houses dating back to the pre-Georgian seventeenth century. This vernacular source became an important inspiration for the *Shingle Style*—a term coined retrospectively by architectural historian Vincent Scully in the 1950s to describe a new American fashion of the 1870s, calmer and more rustic than Queen Anne. Scully gave it a splendid label: "The Architecture of the American Summer." When Cass Gilbert vacationed on Nantucket in the summer of 1879, the shingled architecture of that island, weathering to a silver gray in the salt air since the 1670s, gave him his first sustained exposure to the Shingle Style.[7]

When Cass signed on as Stanford White's assistant in September 1880, McKim, Mead and White was pursuing a loose mix of Queen Anne, colonial, and Shingle Style projects for suburban homes and summer retreats along the East Coast. The most notable project of them all was the Newport Casino (1879–81), which went far to glamorize the Shingle Style for the wealthy summer crowd at the most elegant ocean resort on the Atlantic shore. The casino, anticipating the American country club, was an informal, sprawling pleasure palace for Rhode Island's rich vacationers. It encircled a cropped green space for tournament tennis of national renown. Commissioned by the imperious Manhattan publisher James Gordon Bennett, the casino was still on the drafting boards at 57 Broadway when Cass arrived in 1880. By mutual agreement among the principals at McKim, Mead and White, the work of the firm in its first years remained just that, rather than being credited to a single designer. Both White and McKim involved their assistants in the casino project, and the entire office shared and celebrated its success. Cass remembered joining the job in progress soon after he entered the firm. It was his working introduction to the Shingle Style.[8]

The shingle-clad casino, centrally located near the neck of the Newport peninsula along Bellevue Avenue, inspired a migration of Shingle Style summer places southward on the avenue and along the Newport Cliff Walk overlooking the Atlantic surf. Neighboring the casino on Bellevue was McKim, Mead and White's influential Edna Villa, but the largest and most elaborate of their new rustic "cottages" was "Southside" (1882–84), looking out across its broad velvet greensward toward the Cliff Walk and the ocean. Built for Manhattan realtor and socialite Robert Goelet, Southside was replete with multiple gables, deep porches, and cone-topped bays, all wrapped in a shingle skin. Cass worked on Southside in spring 1882. It was a majestic precedent for the smaller Shingle Style country places that he would design for affluent Twin Cities vacationers on White Bear Lake a few years later. Meanwhile, tycoon James Gordon Bennett, mightily pleased with his Newport Casino, asked McKim, Mead and White to design the interior of his next indulgence, a 226-foot personal steam yacht to be named *Namouna.* Cass happily joined in the work on that. In the process he learned something not only about the architecture of pure luxury but also about the arrogance of power among money-saturated clients, an aspect of his calling which would bother him often in future years.[9]

Soon after Cass signed on at 57 Broadway, he met Stanford White's close friend Augustus Saint-Gaudens. Still in his early thirties, Saint-Gaudens was not yet widely known for the talent that

Augustus Saint-Gaudens, 1880.
(U.S. Department of the Interior, National Park Service, Saint-Gaudens National Historic Site, Cornish, NH)

Colonial style, John Paul Jones House, Portsmouth, New Hampshire, 1758.
(Photo by Ralph Morang)

Shingle Style, Sheldon-Hawkes House, Deerfield, Massachusetts, 1743.
(Photograph by Amanda Merullo. Courtesy of Historic Deerfield, Inc.)

Newport (Rhode Island) Casino, McKim, Mead and White, 1879–81.
(Photo by author)

Edna Villa, Newport, Rhode Island, McKim, Mead and White, 1881–83.
(Photo by author)

would soon propel him to fame as America's finest sculptor. He was struggling with two challenges at the time—the Manhattan statue of Admiral David Farragut, for which White would provide a stunning pedestal, and from which Saint-Gaudens's reputation would take off, and a lesser but more troublesome commission, the statue of an eighteenth-century merchant sailor, Robert Richard Randall, for a site at Sailors' Snug Harbor on Staten Island. After designing a pedestal for this statue, White gave Cass the task of rendering a watercolor sketch combining statue and pedestal for presentation to the client. The assignment was discouraging; Cass was not greatly skilled in drawing human figures. Saint-Gaudens happened by 57 Broadway one day to find White casting a critical eye over Cass's sketch, while Cass stood alongside bracing for judgment. (White had a reputation for explosive reactions to the work of his assistants. "That is the goddamdest lookin' thing I ever saw!" was characteristic, another draftsman recalled.) According to Gilbert, Saint-Gaudens rescued him by offering to draw the statue himself. After a spell of sketching, smudging, and erasing, the sculptor snorted, "Oh Hell, Stan! Nobody can draw it—Give me a bit of clay and I'll model it!" Cass dated his enduring affection for Saint-Gaudens from that moment.[10]

Though he worked up some quiet reservations about White's character during twenty-seven months under his wing, Cass shared the awe of his contemporaries for White's ebullient nature and artistic genius. Late in life he recalled that three men had influenced him more than any others. His young friend Clarence Johnston taught him the "joy of work;" Theodore Roosevelt inspired him to think "free from the trammels of the commonplace;" and White "taught me to *choose* and . . . to think quick." In a long memorandum of 1927 Gilbert elaborated on his memories of White:

> His mind was alert and keen, his decisions prompt and effective, his solutions of difficult problems ingenious, swift and adequate and always in the direction of simplicity. . . . [He] would linger lovingly over some composition of architectural grouping, sketching at first a few faint lines and then suddenly "seeing" his motif,

> as it were, would swiftly strike in the dominant lines of the composition, with just a suggestion of a detail here and there—and behold there was before you just the picturesque mass of chimneys, dormers, roofs and gables needed to fit into the landscape where the building was to go. . . . He was essentially a free master of the picturesque.[11]

The phrase "just the picturesque mass of chimneys, dormers, roofs and gables needed to fit into the landscape" captured an aspect of White's artistry that Gilbert would practice with a striking flair in his own career—a fondness for the scenographic, defining the forms of a building in terms of the "scene" or "picture" it cast from its setting to engage its viewers, rather than stressing interior function or spatial flow. Practitioners of scenographic architecture dominated the American field in the late nineteenth and early twentieth centuries. Gilbert pursued it with conviction, whether working in a picturesque or classical mode. He learned the art from Stanford White.[12]

Gilbert also remembered vividly the sudden long hours that White could commit to a job, forcing his draftsmen to labor unexpectedly far into the night. But their days and nights could fill with youthful pleasures as well. Summer pickup baseball games enlivened the life of the staff. So did good long lubricated lunches at local restaurants. Both sorts of contests left fond memories. Old Tom's tavern, just off lower Broadway on Thames Street, was a favored noontime retreat. One veteran of 57 Broadway remembered that its "mutton chops two inches thick, musty ale, and mince pie with a 'slip-on' of melted cheese, were the order of the day." He added that when the ale flowed more freely than usual, he and his friends would return to the office "quite nicely plastered."[13]

It is hard to imagine Cass plastered. He certainly enjoyed a hearty meal of meat and drink, and years later he cited Old Tom's as a special landmark of his "bohemian" days in New York. But his taste in extracurricular fun tended to be less subversive than drunken afternoons in the office. He lived on Irving Place near Union Square with Clarence Johnston and Frank Bacon. In a letter to Bacon in 1927 he recalled that "nearly 50 years have passed since you sat up in bed at

#40 Irving Place and played the flute (or tried to) and Clarence threw a shoe at you to make you stop, and I looked on and laughed." His personal life was rarely more wicked than that.[14]

Forty Irving Place acquired some fame as the birthplace of the Architectural League of New York, an organization awaiting a long and august future. Even before Cass had returned from Europe, Johnston and a few new acquaintances in the city had patched together a small architectural sketch club, which met at 40 Irving Place. After Gilbert joined them in the late summer of 1880, the sketch club took on a more competitive edge, and in January 1881 it was formalized (at Gilbert's initiative, he later claimed) into the Architectural League, featuring design competitions judged by prominent architects in the city. The results of one such competition, for a narrow row house façade, appeared in the April 16, 1881, issue of *American Architect and Building News*. Gilbert's competition entry was included, its appearance very similar to the street façade of the Charles Barney house that Gilbert was working on in the drafting room at 57 Broadway. At age twenty-one he was published at last.[15]

Meanwhile, the expanding membership of the Architectural League moved into a new clubroom on Fourteenth Street. The room's dark red walls were soon lined with photographs and casts and members' sketches, its air clouded with blue cigar smoke through endless meetings devoted to passionate quarrels over style. To win publicity for the league, Cass persuaded Richard Watson Gilder, editor of *Century Magazine*, to publish a long friendly article illustrated with the work of league members. The article featured a sketch by Cass of an old towered gateway, rendered on his summer walk across France in 1880. Gilder later printed a piece in *Century* by Richard Grant White, Stanford White's father, about the houses of old New York, illustrated with several sketches by league members, including three interiors by Gilbert. Cass's hand-drawn artistry was making a small but satisfying mark.[16]

In spring 1882 Gilbert was dispatched to Baltimore to supervise the construction of a large freestanding urban home for railroader Ross Winans. A Baltimore reporter called it "probably the most costly and elaborate residence ever erected here"—smooth exterior walls of brownstone and brick rising from the sidewalk, and elaborate interiors of oak, teak, and mahogany. The Winans house was an important commission for McKim, Mead and White, and their choice of Gilbert to see it through reflected the confidence and credit he had built up in the office. The assignment gave him crucial hands-on training in the more technical aspects of the construction process, as well as useful face-to-face experience in dealing with the contractor and his small army of sub-contractors as he drove home detailed on-site decisions about the plans worked up at 57 Broadway by McKim and White. Gilbert asserted his artistic autonomy by designing an ornamental fountain wall and basin for the terraced garden behind the Winans house.[17]

Cass worked himself ragged on the Winans project but enjoyed the task quite thoroughly. In letters to Clarence, high morale swept over every obstacle he described. Subcontractors were the special victims of his buoyant scorn. The plumber, he wrote, intended to install "an un Christian arrangement for pulling air out of plumbing pipes. . . . The heater man is another headstrong emissary of the evil one and is linked with the plumber, the gas fitter and the lightning rod man in an unholy conspiracy to wreck the looks of the house." So it went with the stair builder, the plasterer, the electric-bell man, the cabinetmaker, the stonecutter, each of them a barrier to aesthetic progress. Cass had been told that finishing the house on schedule was impossible. But he assured Clarence that "if gut and energy with hard work will do it—she's going to be finished sure." In the end, the client Winans was thoroughly pleased and rewarded Cass with an invitation to visit his summer place in Newport as a house guest.[18]

The interlude in Baltimore was refreshing for Cass in other ways. He was glad to be out from under the thumb of Stanford White and in charge of his own hours. In fact, the liberties of the Winans job spoiled him for a return to 57 Broadway. He improved his time with weekend jaunts into the Maryland countryside to savor the gentle green landscape and its country homes. During one bright Sunday stroll west of the city he came upon a beautiful old colonial house called Doughoregan Manor, once owned by Charles Carroll of Carrollton, a signer of the Declaration of Independence. The Carrolls had been among the founders and leading landowners of pre-Revolutionary Maryland. The manor, built in 1727, is a large brick plantation house laid out in the Chesapeake manner, with a big central living block flanked by dependencies on either side. Cass looked it over with great care, admiring its precise axial symmetry and fine Georgian interiors.

He was so taken by the place that he asked White for ten days off with pay to sketch it, make measured drawings, and take casts of the interior woodwork. Apparently nothing came of this proposal—completion of the Winans house took priority—but Cass's encounter with Doughoregan Manor marked the onset of his personal affection for eighteenth-century American Georgian architecture.[19]

Doughoregan Manor, 1727.
(From John H. Scarff, editor, The Bicentenary Celebration of the Birth of Charles Carroll of Carrollton, 1737–1937 *[n.p., 1937])*

His trips from Baltimore back to the home office at 57 Broadway confirmed in Cass the feeling that he had "run the scale" with McKim, Mead and White. It was time, he decided, to get on with his career elsewhere. The mood of the office had chilled a bit, he confided to Clarence, who had now gone home to begin his own practice in St. Paul. Cass's good opinion of Stanford White had also cooled:

> Mr. White of course is a man to be admired for his ability, we both understand that; but in the last few months I have heard things and observed things in his private character that make me respect him none the more. I believe he is my friend at the moment . . . but I am getting a little sick of his arrogance, and his claiming all the credit for everything done in his office. A man likes to have a little of the praise his work receives for himself and not given to others. And I believe if Mr. White thought any of the fellows were getting glory out of the work he'd be down on them at once.[20]

This was more than the grumbling of a restless draftsman. The shift of attitude toward White that Cass confessed stemmed from a new friendship he struck up at 57 Broadway with Joseph M. Wells, who had recently returned to the office from a long tour of Europe.

Joseph Wells, ca. 1880s.
(From Charles Baldwin, Stanford White *[New York: Dodd, Mead, 1931])*

Wells became the most influential architect in the firm below the partners and helped nudge it toward neoclassicism in the 1880s. A brilliant, introverted man with a bent for caustic opinions delivered with a saving gentle wit, he managed to command the affection of both White and Gilbert. This was the more remarkable in Gilbert's case, since Wells was a religious skeptic with bluntly unconventional social views. He once challenged the pious contemporary notion that cleanliness was next to godliness with a splendid claim that "prostitutes are, physically, the cleanest persons alive" in New York City. He enjoyed startling Cass with such observations and laced his letters with fine gossip about White's notorious sex life. When White married in 1884, Wells wrote that "the novelty of it is probably already over, and perhaps things can be tided over tolerably until the usual event happens." Wells also shared Cass's growing resentment over White's habit of assuming credit for the work of his assistants.[21]

Another factor feeding Cass's restlessness was the lure of St. Paul, where both his mother and now Clarence Johnston tugged at him. Clarence and Cass were still "best friends," and Clarence's return to St. Paul in 1882 stirred in Cass the idea of going home to set up practice with him, a notion that had been playing on his mind for some time. Meanwhile, his mother made plain her yearning for the return of her favorite son. In a self-pitying birthday letter to Cass in January 1882 she wrote, "I am made to realize more fully than ever that the home nest is forever broken up and you will probably never all gather round me except when I am in my coffin." The son vowed to scotch this glum prediction and began laying plans to restore the nest. While in Baltimore he worked out the design of a new home for his mother, to be located in the neighborhood of Summit Avenue in St. Paul, with the hope of one day moving into it with her. The maternal pull was that strong.[22]

But mainly Cass hungered now for the chance to assert his talent on his own. In Baltimore he had demonstrated his competence beyond the drafting room, and he was poised for the next big steps. He said as much to Stanford White, and White agreed. In December 1882, shortly after his twenty-third birthday, he followed Johnston home to practice architecture in St. Paul. His chum at 57 Broadway, Joseph M. Wells, who had never ventured west of Hoboken, sent him a characteristic farewell:

> I have the suspicion that Religion in the West [is] sufficient indeed to enkindle a small conflagration in the souls of your fellow townsmen. Preach against the vain and senseless trappings of vanity and folly—balls, parties, late suppers, dress coats, painted shoes, aesthetic cravats, arabesques (of all the maladies surely the sorest). I wish you God speed. As for me, I am wallowing deeper and deeper in the quagmire of atheism.[23]

Cass welcomed Wells's poking wit. Nine months in Boston, eight months in Europe, and twenty-seven months in New York, Newport, and Baltimore had etched some changes in the youngster who had left St. Paul in 1878 to become an architect. He had now savored a world of free artistic self-expression and cultural emancipation that would remain unforgettable. He knew his way around and had grown to enjoy the artist's urban liberties. "I loved the excitement and the pleasures of life in New York," he would confess to a Manhattan friend a few years later, "the opportunities for advancement, the pursuit of ambition, the theaters, the places of amusement, and such nights as the last one I spent with you just as I was leaving for the West. I did not want to give them up. . . ." But Wells's wry intuition about Cass at the time was accurate nevertheless. The child of the Midwest—the churchgoing son of Zanesville, the earnest young Minnesota striver—had by no means disappeared. His ambition for advancement remained sharp and purposeful, but for the moment he chose to go home and pursue it in familiar territory.[24]

As the years passed, his regret over leaving 57 Broadway turned into pure nostalgia over having once been there. "I never was more happy in my life than in the old office and I can tell you that means a good deal for I have had a happy life," he wrote in 1911 near the peak of his career. "What a loveable crowd it was—what fine fellows, and how proud I was to be one of them. There was nothing better than . . . that joyous devotion to our work—that happiness."

Nostalgia and all, this was telling testimony by a now famous architect about an important source of his success. However, in 1882, as he headed home to St. Paul, success still shimmered far out ahead of him, elusive and well beyond his reach.[25]

5

Starting Out in St. Paul

Cass launched his Minnesota practice in January 1883 in a small office in the newly completed Gilfillan block in downtown St. Paul. His two closest boyhood friends, Clarence Johnston and James Knox Taylor, kept offices in the same six-story building, both having returned from Manhattan several months earlier. The three friends joined a small crowd of young architects in the Twin Cities in the early 1880s, each poised to exploit the spectacular economic takeoff of the region that followed the bleak depression years of the 1870s.[1]

American cities grew faster than any others in the world in the 1880s, and the Twin Cities kept pace among them. Together they boasted a population of 87,000 in 1880. A decade later that number had shot to 298,000. A local newspaper report of October 1883 placed St. Paul fourth in the country in dollar value of new construction, led only by New York City, Chicago, and Cincinnati. Eastern investment capital fueled the St. Paul boom, and the young eastern-trained architects jostled with local old-timers as well as engineers and contractors for a share in the profits. Minneapolis outstripped St. Paul's population growth rate, rising "like an exhalation" (Montgomery Schuyler's phrase) on the strength of its vigorous milling industry, but St. Paul's cramped downtown geography along the Mississippi River encouraged taller office buildings. St. Paul also led its rival by a healthy margin in saloons and legalized brothels. And nothing in the residential districts of Minneapolis could match the allure of St. Paul's magnificent Summit Avenue ridge above its downtown, where prospering lawyers, bankers, and other urban professionals searched for home sites to match their pocketbooks.[2]

Technology melded St. Paul's commercial core with its residential sanctuary on the Summit Avenue ridge more conveniently with every passing year. The pace of progress downtown and along the ridge was relentless. Gaslit street lamps arrived in 1867; a municipal water system in 1869, followed by sewers in 1873; horse-drawn streetcars in 1872; street paving (with wooden blocks) in 1873; telephone service in 1877; electric arc street lights in 1883; asphalt paving on Summit Avenue in 1887; steam cable cars in 1888, soon replaced by electric trolleys in the early 1890s. These advances promoted both a crowded inner city and a broadening urban rim. As commuting began to scatter the homes of the downtown white-collar working population, business and professional decision making centered ever more compactly in high-rise office space at the core.[3]

In the tall new buildings downtown, technology was also changing the nature of office work. Typewriters, telephones, flush toilets, and the electric elevator (replacing its steam-powered predecessor) began to modernize the daily routine of white-collar employees. Meanwhile, offices filled with a rising percentage of young women—mostly self-respecting graduates of the new municipal high schools, well dressed, underpaid, emancipated from their household role as dutiful daughters to become dutiful clerks. They made up the fastest growing segment of the downtown office work force.

Meanwhile, in the big new homes out on the ridge, domestic work was becoming somewhat easier physically and a lot more complex socially. Hot and cold running water arrived, along with ever more elaborate parlors, dining rooms, and kitchens, illuminated by gas, kerosene, and then the first rudiments of electricity. (In many homes gas lighting was retained to back up unreliable electric wiring systems well past the turn of the century.) Together these technological strides turned the upper-middle-class wife into a household manager, responsible for the good appearance of every visible interior space, the pleasant presentation of every meal, and the efficient conduct of every white-starched servant on her domestic work force—preferably Swedish, German if necessary, Irish if it came to that.[4]

Some nagging realities would not go away. Everywhere in this modernizing urban world, downtown and up on the ridge, the pale outdoor aroma of street manure and the indoor buzz of the common fly remained pervasive. The horseless carriage and the perfect window screen (along with the mitigation of fire, pestilence, pollution, and poverty) awaited a still more progressive future. But for those who profited from urban growth on the terms of the day, or wanted to, the 1880s seemed like a bright bonanza. Each new year promised to be better than the last.[5]

For young architects on the rise, the best commissions were those landed for the basic institutional structures demanded by fast city growth—office buildings, warehouses, schools, libraries, rail stations, and a whole new generation of urban churches. These were mostly big buildings with predictable interior spaces. The clients who wanted them were equipped with firm budgets and businesslike committees responsive to the needs of large groups of anonymous users. Architectural solutions for projects of this sort tended to emerge from relatively efficient tabletop negotiation. The clients were often in a hurry, and the fees could be quite substantial.

The private residence was another matter, its multiple functions more subtle. Middle-class homes had emerged nationwide across the pre–Civil War decades as personalized centers for American family aspiration. Parents wanted their houses to somehow enforce the virtues of Christian morality brought home from church and Sunday school. They also wanted the house to fortify a firm domestic hierarchy among family members and their servants. Meanwhile, it had to service the urge for seclusion and relief from the life of the street and the downtown job. And beyond its roles as training center and sanctuary, the house became a crucial social statement aimed at neighbors, passersby, and invited guests about the status and taste of its occupants. This meant important choices about style, ornament, and decor, indoors and out. The parameters of cost for such a home were very elastic, with final price tags dependent on protracted family decision making. Calculations and desires wobbled endlessly.

The emotional investment in a new home was often larger than the dollar investment a family could actually afford. Gilbert recalled how often these considerations curbed his design ambitions: "All my designs were made to suit the special requirements of my clients, and represent conditions and arrangements for economy that relate to the particular instances in hand." For an architect seeking success, planning a residence for an upwardly mobile family could be among the most complex diplomatic challenges of his young career.[6]

Gilbert and his young St. Paul colleagues scrambled for every plausible commission, public or private, institutional or residential. To this competition, Cass brought some serious disadvantages. His credentials in St. Paul were not nearly as well known as those of Clarence Johnston, whose father was a gifted journalist rubbing shoulders with state and local politicians, or Jim Taylor, the son of a wealthy realtor and trustee of St. Paul's Macalester College. Johnston started winning house commissions from prosperous businessmen soon after his return to St. Paul in summer 1882. Later that fall, contemplating at last a trip abroad, he invited Cass to fill in as his office manager. Cass declined. In fact the offer and its refusal cast a pall over their friendship that never quite lifted. Cass intended to make it on his own, not as the employee of a boyhood friend.[7]

He hoped from the outset that his connection with McKim, Mead and White would bring him work from the Northern Pacific Railroad, since the ambitious president of Northern Pacific, Henry Villard, had close ties with 57 Broadway. While Cass was still working there, Stanford White had begun designing a lordly complex of six townhouses for Villard on Madison Avenue, and Cass's friend Joseph Wells helped refine this complex into a striking Italian Renaissance palazzo. (It survives today as a luxury hotel, among midtown Manhattan's most elegant residential relics.) Villard also planned to use McKim, Mead and White for a vast expansion of his transcontinental rail empire—depots, hotels, company offices, and hospitals—

from its eastern terminus in St. Paul westward some 2,150 miles to the Pacific Coast. Here was one of those colossal construction projects of the Gilded Age that boggled the minds of potential participants and brought on heavy breathing while they dreamed.

Cass dreamed of heading a St. Paul branch of McKim, Mead and White to help move Villard's grand continental design along. Rarely in his career did Cass dream without purpose. In June 1883 William Mead, in response to a letter from Gilbert, visited St. Paul to explore the notion and put Cass in charge of all the firm's work for Northern Pacific between St. Paul and Helena, Montana, a stretch of 1,200 miles. Elated, Cass promptly took on three draftsmen and went to work. His office hummed for the first time. The immediate task was to supervise the construction of a sprawling company hospital, after plans dispatched from 57 Broadway. The plans called for a big plain institutional version of Southside, the firm's new Shingle Style summer place along the Newport cliffs. Complete with towered bays and enveloping porches, the hospital went up along the Northern Pacific line in Brainerd, Minnesota, where the company maintained a big cluster of machine shops. Cass also supervised completion of the interior of Northern Pacific's new headquarters in St. Paul.[8]

The future seemed to blaze brightly for Cass by September 1883, when completion of Northern Pacific track to the West Coast inspired a rousing celebration in St. Paul. Six huge ceremonial arches graced a long street parade through the city led by President Chester Arthur, General Ulysses Grant, and the main celebrity of the day, capitalist Henry Villard. Young women tossed rose petals at Villard as his carriage rolled by. If Cass were present, he might have tossed a few himself.[9]

Then Villard's empire suddenly collapsed. Northern Pacific's transcontinental leap overstretched his resources, and a run on the company's stock got underway. Creditors closed in on Villard, and in January 1884 he resigned. Gilbert's hope of heading a St. Paul office of McKim, Mead and White to create buildings for Northern Pacific's westward expansion abruptly blinked out. Soon after Villard's resignation, Cass wrote tersely to an English friend about his busted dream: "From a business point of view I am not very prosperous." He added that he had some new "ideas about my profession which perhaps you would not understand (not being an architect)."[10]

His main new idea was to build a broader local base of potential clients. The New York connection having failed him, Cass began patching a network closer to home. He now became an avid St. Paul "club man." In 1884 he helped organize the Minnesota Club, a social rendezvous for the city's professional elite. He was the only architect on the charter list. The club's most prominent member, certainly from Cass's perspective, was the railroader James J. Hill, heir apparent to Henry Villard's shattered empire. In later years Hill would give Cass valuable if sometimes bruising lessons about doing business directly with a powerful millionaire. Meanwhile, membership in the Minnesota Boat Club, and later a golfing club and a tennis club, brought Cass enjoyable exercise, gregarious clubhouse leisure, and new clusters of affluent contacts. This energetic social joining (a durable habit from then on in his career, making him vulnerable to easy criticism) was central to his plans for long-term career advancement.[11]

In 1884, to further improve the reach of his office and its capabilities, he took on James Knox Taylor as a partner. Taylor had collabo-

St. Paul tennis club members, Cass Gilbert in back row, third from left, ca. 1905.
(MHS Collections)

rated with Clarence Johnston on several projects over the previous year and now moved easily from one friend to the other. For Cass the advantages of the new partnership were clear. Taylor, through his father, enjoyed good standing among St. Paul realtors. He brought a shrewd head for business transactions, as well as architectural training roughly the caliber of Cass's own. Beyond that, his personal friendship with Cass proved warm and flexible. No clear line divided their office functions. Both were skilled in cultivating clients. Both enjoyed the work of the drafting room. Both found themselves caught up in the hands-on details of construction oversight, holding contractors to the mark on everything from timber sap to careless plumbing. The evidence suggests, though, that the more creative aspects of office production—especially its residential architecture—fell to Cass, including structural plans, elevations, and the perspective renderings, which he lingered over with passionate care. (He told one client in 1884 that "it is only my desire to do all this work of yours with my own hand instead of having it done by my draughtsman under direction, that has kept it so long delayed.") Meanwhile, Taylor mainly tended to the books and business of the firm. Their partnership ran smoothly for seven years, and their friendship lasted much longer than that.[12]

Cass's first residential creation in St. Paul actually preceded the partnership and his search for new clients. He had returned to St. Paul with a house design for his mother, who by now had gained some affluence from her real estate holdings in the city. He wrote of his plans, "It has become a little problem to do something which shall be artistic, not fashionable, sensible, genuine, and a place I shall not tire of myself." His mother's house turned out to be a fine beginning. Completed in 1883 and still standing at 471 Ashland Avenue, three blocks north of Summit Avenue, it is a modest but inviting gable-roofed home in the Shingle Style with tall dormers and wrapping porch, anticipating several elaborations on this theme that came from his hand in succeeding years. The interior is graced with multiple fireplaces, built-in dining room cabinetry, leaded stained-glass staircase accents, and burnished woodwork. It included space for Cass's own

Gilbert's mother's house, 471 Ashland Avenue, St. Paul, 1883.
(Photo by author)

David McCourt House, 161 Cambridge Street, St. Paul, 1890.
(Photo by author)

bachelor needs, and he moved in with his mother and two brothers when it was ready. (Partner Jim Taylor also moved in for a few months before his marriage in 1887.) The house brought the mother and her favorite son enormous satisfaction. As well it might: together, as client and architect, at 471 Ashland they had introduced the Shingle Style to St. Paul.[13]

In his mother's new neighborhood Gilbert designed similarly unpretentious but nicely crafted homes for physician William Davis (1883), surgeon Archibald McLaren (1886), and banker Everett Bailey (1885), and a more elaborate red-brick house for attorney John White (1885). Gilbert's interior spatial arrangements were not overly adventurous, but in each case careful detailing suited to the client's taste, usually including one or more of Gilbert's innovative recessed fireplaces, enriched the interior. John White had serious reservations about his house at first and had "quite a row" with Cass about it before finally retracting every criticism—much to the relief of Mrs. White, who liked it all along.[14]

The best commission Cass won in his first year of practice was for financier John Q. Adams's mansion. Adams's budget allowed stained glass ("strong and brilliant" but not "gaudy," Cass specified) from New York artist John LaFarge, who had completed his famous frescoes and windows for Richardson's Trinity Church in Boston just a few years before and would help Cass decorate the interior of the new Minnesota State House twenty years later.[15]

Gilbert's most appealing St. Paul Shingle Style venture is a cottage on Cambridge Street built in 1890 for dentist David McCourt—a snug gambrel-roofed home with a crowned corner bay and broad front porch supported by tapering shingled columns. The morning sun casts changing shadow patterns across the front of the McCourt cottage. Saw-tooth edges in the shingled cornice of its corner bay are a characteristic Gilbert detail. Interior space opens in an easy circular flow from room to room, achieving generous surprises for such a compact home.[16]

The chance to explore the larger possibilities of the Shingle Style, as Stanford White had done at Newport and elsewhere, arrived for Gilbert early on, when he was asked to design a big summer home for the Barnum family on White Bear Lake, a popular vacation sanctuary some ten miles north of St. Paul. The Barnum house, built in 1884, destroyed in the 1930s, was the first of several lakeside retreats he designed to grace the summer lives of St. Paul's urban rich. In 1884 Gilbert also designed for lawyer Reuben Galusha a more modest but beautifully detailed shingled cottage that remains intact near the western edge of White Bear Lake. Most of Gilbert's other summerhouses went up on nearby Manitou Island just off the lake's western shore. Those that survive have been decisively modified over the years to meet the demands of year-round living, harsh winter weather, and the automobile. But in scenographic terms they retain the distinction of their origins.

The Jasper Tarbox "cottage" is the oldest of them—a spacious shingle-clad complex, its broad, smooth-flowing gable roof anchored by a prominent cone-crowned bay. The long shadow of H. H. Richardson's influence may be detected in the Tarbox house. As com-

Jasper Tarbox Cottage, ink and wash, Cass Gilbert, 1889.
(Negative number 69633, © Collection of The New-York Historical Society)

pleted in 1889 it bore a remarkable resemblance in concept and finish to Richardson's 1886 Henry Potter house in suburban St. Louis. In 1892 Gilbert designed another large summer home on the island for hardware manufacturer William B. Dean. This commission verified the ongoing success of Gilbert's professional networking. Dean was a director of James J. Hill's Great Northern Railway and a Republican state legislator. In 1893 he introduced the bill authorizing a new state capitol for Minnesota, the project that would transform Gilbert's career. Meanwhile, Dean's son hired Cass to design a home near his father's in St. Paul. The elder Dean's house on Manitou Island today has a decisive neo-Georgian air, enforced by tall columned porticoes, which were probably not a part of the original design. Nearby on the island is Gilbert's most ebullient Shingle Style creation, a summer home for the family of St. Paul clothing dealer James Skinner. Gilbert published what may have been a prototype for this house in *American Architect and Building News* in 1891, and Vincent Scully reprinted it in *The Architecture of the American Summer* a century later. The Skinner house, as finally built in 1895, melded gables, dormers, deep porches, and a hip-roofed porte-cochère with a mix of

Henry S. Potter House, St. Louis, Missouri, H. H. Richardson, 1886.
(Courtesy Missouri Historical Society, St. Louis)

shingled and clapboard surfaces rising from a high foundation of rough-cut stone—a celebration of the stylistic possibilities that Scully's writings have made famous. In the late 1890s, when fortune began to smile on Gilbert's family circumstances, he would retreat to Manitou Island for his own vacations, staying in a remodeled community clubhouse he himself had earlier designed. For all his growing affluence he never enjoyed such princely rustic summer space as he created for his clients on the island.[17]

East Coast architectural shops had promoted the revival of early American architecture since the 1870s, expressed in both the Shingle Style and neo-Georgian creations drawn from eighteenth-century examples. True to his training at McKim, Mead and White, Cass Gilbert proceeded to bring the neo-Georgian look to St. Paul, as he had the Shingle Style. A widely influential model of neo-Georgian styling was Charles McKim's design, begun in 1882 when Cass was still with the New York firm, for H. A. C. Taylor's mansion in Newport, finally completed in 1886. Alert to its importance, Gilbert worked up a compact interpretation of the Taylor house for St. Paul wholesale pharmacist Charles P. Noyes on Virginia Street, just off

James Skinner House, Manitou Island, 1895.
(Photo by author)

H. A. C. Taylor Mansion, Newport, Rhode Island, Charles McKim, 1886.
(Courtesy Newport Historical Society)

Charles P. and Emily Noyes House, 89 Virginia Street, St. Paul, 1887.
(MHS Collections)

Summit Avenue. Noyes and his wife were avid participants in the design process. "Saturday evening James and I had to go up to the Noyes' and talk house with them," Cass told a friend a bit impatiently. "We got there at eight o'clock, and will you believe it, we were kept until five minutes after twelve."[18]

The Noyes house, finished in 1887, is a diligent exercise in Georgian symmetry—Palladian window over the central entry porch, four massive chimneys rising from a hip roof, narrow clapboard siding, and a porte-cochère. Its appearance fortified Gilbert's rising reputation as a master of disciplined stylistic nuance. Nearby variants on the neo-Georgian theme soon followed, for steel executive Howard Elmer, a close personal friend; for William J. Dean, son and partner of the hardware manufacturer William B. Dean; and for attorney Emerson Hadley.

In a breakthrough of sorts, Gilbert and Taylor landed their first Summit Avenue commission in 1886 when law partners William Lightner and George Young, downtown office neighbors of the architects in the Gilfillan block, asked for a double house—unusual in Midwestern cities—to go up near the eastern crest of the avenue. The response was a stone complex of rock-faced jasper, two homes distinct but compatible, seamed by a common wall, in the style loosely known today as Richardsonian Romanesque. This was Gilbert and Taylor's most lucrative residential commission yet. They added another house to Summit Avenue—an even more costly Romanesque mansion of red sandstone and brick for railroad magnate Edgar Long—before agreeing to end their partnership in 1891.

In the 1890s Cass designed six more homes for the avenue. The most arresting of these was the William Lightner house, built in 1893 for the lawyer whose family had outgrown its half of the 1886 Lightner-Young double house next door. The new Lightner house is a blocky hip-roofed residential fortress of rock-faced jasper set off by brownstone banding and a round-arched Richardsonian entry of massive brownstone wedges. The symmetrical arrangements of the Lightner house façade derive from Gilbert's initial proposal, rejected by the Lightners, for a neoclassical design, complete with Corinthian porch columns and corner pilasters. As built, the house remains Gilbert's strongest Richardsonian offering to his hometown. The Lightners lived in it for over forty years. Viewed from the avenue, its appearance is similar to Richardson's design for the 1888 St. Louis residence, since destroyed, of J. R. Lionberger—the last of the master's rare ventures into symmetry before he died.[19]

Gilbert's Summit Avenue homes made up a substantial legacy, but their number was modest next to that of his one-time friend Clarence Johnston, who enjoyed the more resounding success in snaring residential commissions after he and Cass became rivals in the 1880s. Johnston completed eighteen Summit Avenue residences before 1900 and fifteen more thereafter. He was clearly the architect of choice for St. Paul's Summit Avenue elite. His clients tended to be very rich, and his houses for them heavily eclectic. Johnston's early work, compared with Gilbert's, was less disciplined in layout and more indulgent in stylistic flourish. It set a tone that later inspired such disparate critics as F. Scott Fitzgerald (who grew up near Summit Avenue) and Frank Lloyd Wright—both scornful of dated archi-

Edgar C. Long House, 332 Summit Avenue, St. Paul, Gilbert and Taylor, 1890. *(MHS Collections)*

William H. Lightner and George B. Young double house, 322-324 Summit Avenue, St. Paul, Gilbert and Taylor, 1886.
(MHS Collections)

William H. Lightner House, 318 Summit Avenue, St. Paul, 1893.
(Photo by Thomas Lutz, MHS Collections)

William H. Lightner House, perspective drawing, Cass Gilbert, 1893.
(Negative number 63635, © Collection of The New-York Historical Society)

John R. Lionberger House, St. Louis, Missouri, H. H. Richardson, 1888.
(Courtesy Missouri Historical Society, St. Louis)

tectural opulence—to regard the avenue, in Fitzgerald's words, as a "museum of American architectural failures." Nevertheless, Gilbert's and Johnston's mansions together helped make the avenue a thriving rival of Cleveland's Euclid Avenue and Chicago's Prairie Avenue as a residential showcase of the urban Midwest at the turn of the century. And in striking contrast to Euclid and Prairie Avenues, St. Paul's Summit Avenue remains intact today as a living residential neighborhood.[20]

In later years Gilbert referred to the 1880s as "the days when I was building houses." He eventually created over two dozen of them for St. Paul. He also designed five churches in the area flanking Summit Avenue. The largest of them was the 1886 Dayton Avenue Presbyterian Church, his mother's church. As a founding member of the congregation, she had a hand in the choice of her son as architect. Cass was no longer much of a churchgoer, but he had a sure sense of what he wanted to build. "I was brought up a Presbyterian myself," he wrote, "so I know the needs are principally for a simple auditorium." A radial seating plan under a vaulted ceiling with timber support ribs encouraged the worshippers' undistracted concentration on altar and pulpit. H. H. Richardson's two churches in Springfield, Massachusetts, influenced Gilbert's Dayton Avenue exterior. Critic Montgomery Schuyler looked it over on a visit to St. Paul in 1891 and announced his measured approval, though he clearly preferred Richardson's Springfield spires. Gilbert's psychological investment in his church was strong. While its construction was underway, he enjoyed viewing it after dark—"over to Dayton Ave past the walls of our stone church—grey—mysterious in the moonlight." He clad the roof of the church with red slate, a colorful Mediterranean touch he would employ elsewhere in later years. It recalled the mellow red-tile roofs he encountered everywhere in Italy during his trip abroad in 1880.[21]

Gilbert's nearby Virginia Street Church, a picturesque miniature for St. Paul's Swedenborgians, also went up in 1886. Its lower walls are lined with river boulders, and it is crowned by a charming little spire that flares out like a witch's hat over a shingle-clad octagonal tower. (Gilbert returned to this theme more than once. In 1898 he created a larger version of the Virginia Street tower-and-spire for a remarkable Shingle Style Episcopal church in Moorhead on the Red River, the last of a dozen Minnesota churches he designed before leaving the state.)[22]

Gilbert's offering of 1887 is another shingled miniature, Camp Memorial Chapel (now St. Martin's by the Lake), a fetching masterpiece in the beauty of its symmetry, small gabled dormers, and gently flaring roofs. This Episcopal church is located at Lafayette Bay on Lake Minnetonka west of Minneapolis, a site that registered the young architect's reach into yet another summer sanctuary of the Twin Cities' elite.[23]

The German Bethlehem Presbyterian Church, built at the foot of the bluff below Summit Avenue in 1890 for a congregation of German immigrants, is Gilbert's most innovative religious structure. He enjoyed returning to see it year after year into the new century, until the congregation was forcibly disbanded during the anti-German passions of World War I. The church is wonderfully site-specific, nestled against its bluff and rising in a picturesque variety of shapes and textures. It has the fairy-tale look of a small castle, and a winding stone staircase ascending to its entry enhances the romance. Its changing secular uses in the twentieth century never diminished its visual appeal.[24]

In 1894 Mrs. Theodore Eaton, widow of a former rector of St. Clement's Episcopal Church in St. Paul, gave $25,000 in memory of her husband for a new sanctuary a block off Summit Avenue at the then western edge of the area's development. Gilbert's design for the exterior is a handsome Romanesque variant of English Gothic revival styling. Dark timber tracery around the main entry rests against low walls of ashlar masonry. The donor's largesse and her demanding attention to interior detail drew Cass ever closer to the project as it neared completion. He sketched patterns for its stained glass windows and personally painted the decorations around its altar. Writing thirty-six years later about the church, and about subsequent additions he disliked, he fumed: "St. Clement's Church was a labor of

Dayton Avenue Presbyterian Church, St. Paul, 1886.
(MHS Collections)

Virginia Street Church (Swedenborgian), 170 Virginia Street, St. Paul, 1886.
(Photo by Diana Mitchell, MHS Collections)

German Bethlehem Presbyterian Church,
311 Ramsey Street, St. Paul, 1890.
(Photo by author)

St. Clement's Church,
Portland and Milton, St. Paul, 1894.
(MHS Collections)

love. It was something more than a mere 'job.' It was a thing that engaged my full endeavor and had come to mean a spiritual idea. Whoever had charge of the work subsequently certainly could have had no conception of how I feel about it. . . . [An] architect's interest in his work is the same as that of a painter of a picture or the writer of a poem, and it ought not to be altered or marred by other hands." This angry lament was the most heartfelt statement Gilbert ever made about the architect as artist, supremely concerned with the integrity of his creations.[25]

Early on, Gilbert and Taylor's practice began reaching out beyond the Twin Cities to smaller places in Minnesota, Wisconsin, the Dakotas, and as far west as Helena, Montana, a prospering territorial capital and mining center, which had been linked to St. Paul by rail in 1883. Despite the westward momentum of the iron horse, getting across Montana to its capital could still be a frontier adventure. In March 1887 Cass headed for Helena by train toward the end of the hardest winter in anyone's memory. Ice chunks in the flooded Missouri River blocked the tracks near Bismarck, North Dakota. Cass and his fellow passengers crossed the river by boat to climb into a cluster of old stagecoaches on the other side. The stage drivers then began an exuberant race westward over the frozen prairie toward the next train stop, and found themselves galloping through a sudden blizzard. Since Gilbert's stage was filled with women and children, he sat up on the box with the driver. Suddenly the driver lost control of his charging team. The coach spilled over, and Cass and the driver were thrown into the fresh snow. The driver was badly injured but Cass got up unhurt and ran to help the other passengers. The nasty accident had a happy ending. Wagons and doctors finally arrived, and injuries were treated. Survivors caught the next train west, and Cass met his appointments in Helena two days later. Territorial newspapers carried the dramatic tale. Cass saved the clippings.[26]

His main client in Helena was a Jewish banker, Albert J. Seligman, scion of a rich and distinguished international family, for whom Cass designed a big rambling residence mixing Queen Anne and colonial with the Shingle Style—probably the first such combination in Montana—while negotiating several downtown business projects with him. Cass was not immune to the anti-Semitism spreading westward from the Atlantic seaboard in the 1880s, but he enjoyed his friendship with the cultivated Helena banker. "I must say if all his race were as generous and broad-minded as Seligman I should lose my prejudice completely," he told a friend. As it worked out in later years, Gilbert's anti-Semitism would intensify rather than fade in the teeth of rising Jewish immigration from the *shtetls* of Eastern Europe. But along with many other genteel anti-Semites of his generation, Cass learned to cope with the troubling identity of particular clients, colleagues, and craftsmen with an earnest cordiality and respect. And he never lost his admiration for Seligman. In fact, two decades after designing a home for him in Helena, Cass would choose Seligman as his personal financial adviser after both men had moved to New York City.[27]

By the early 1890s Gilbert had established a reputation as perhaps the most talented, energetic, and disciplined young architect among the batch that had gathered in the Twin Cities a decade earlier to exploit rapid urban growth. In July 1886 a prominent French architectural journal, *La Semaine des Constructeurs,* published one of his St. Paul residential designs to illustrate and endorse the current state of architectural practice in America. Cass had brought the eastern newness to a region aching for cultural maturity, and he brought it at a level of surpassing quality. Furthermore, for all their eagerness to win in the hustle for affluent clients, he and partner Jim Taylor combined in their work an artistic integrity coupled with unquestioned business probity—no mean feat in the commercial whirligig of the 1880s. But Cass wanted more.

Part of what he wanted might well have reached him from the pages of a favorite novel, William Dean Howells's *The Rise of Silas Lapham*, published in 1885, a Boston success story grounded in the ironic realities of what success demanded from men on the make. But Howells's main message about the rise—and fall—of paint dealer Silas Lapham apparently interested Gilbert less than the novel's architectural detail. Howells had Lapham clinch his success by building a new home for himself on "the water side of Beacon," designed by an architect who guided his client away from the conventional excesses of the Gilded Age, including heavy high-studded walls of black walnut, toward brighter and simpler, more "modern" interior spaces.

When he read the novel, Gilbert must have known that Howells was the brother-in-law of William Rutherford Mead, the architect who brought Gilbert into the firm of McKim, Mead and White. Less certain is whether Gilbert knew that Howells himself had resided in a suburban Boston home designed by Mead and was living on the water side of Beacon when he wrote the novel. In any event, three decades later in March 1917 Gilbert announced that Howells had done more to cultivate good taste in American architecture than any living architect. "A single sentence in 'Silas Lapham' about black walnut," he wrote, "changed the entire trend of thought, and made it possible for the architects of the time to stem the torpid tide of brownstone and black walnut then so dear to the heart of the American millionaire." In the 1880s Gilbert ranked himself among the young architects who integrated new directions and introduced them to their wealthy clients. He wanted to share the fullest rewards of recognition for doing so.[28]

In fall 1886, at age twenty-six, he candidly confessed that he had been bitten by that pervasive nemesis of his era, what William James would one day call the American "bitch-goddess success." Cass defined his case precisely. Unlike Silas Lapham he did not crave the sort of success that meant "the worldly pursuit of worldly advancement alone." Rather, he wanted a "position in the world which will increase my chances of getting great work to do, and of having the influence to carry it out." His goal was "to stand not only well in, but at the head of my profession."[29]

These were pretty unguarded ambitions. Cass chose to share them with a young woman from Milwaukee named Julia Finch. Earlier that autumn, he had fallen in love with her.

6

Falling in Love

Julia Finch crossed paths with Cass late in the summer of 1886, while vacationing near the Twin Cities at Lake Minnetonka. They walked the Minnetonka beach together looking for lucky stones. They dug holes in the sand and went boating. "What a happy day that was," Cass later mused, "with all the sweet uncertainty of love half confessed."

They had first met in New York City back in 1880, when Cass was working at 57 Broadway and Julia was attending Miss Chapman's finishing school. Cass called her "my New York girl." After polishing by Miss Chapman she had toured Europe with her parents, studied music in Chicago, and become a practicing Christian. Now, six years later, she was a mature young woman of twenty-four, straightforward and unaffected in social situations, strong-willed, saucy, and pretty—"stunningly pretty," a bachelor friend reported. She lived in Milwaukee with her mother and younger sister. Her father, a prominent Wisconsin attorney, had died the year before, leaving them in narrower circumstances than they had expected. They had been "in society" before her father died but now rarely went calling. Julia gave piano lessons in her home and sang solos in church on Sunday. On summer holidays she played tennis and enjoyed sailing. She entertained a steady run of suitors, but none of them interested her very much. She was beginning to think she might never marry.[1]

Julia Finch, ca. 1880–85.
(MHS Collections)

Falling in love, when it happened, was quick and easy for both. "The knowledge that I was in love came upon me with such overwhelming suddenness," Julia told Cass a few weeks later, "that it took my breath away and I have been rather gasping ever since." This sort of confession was squarely in line with the established middle-class romantic mating rituals of the 1880s. Following the sequence of these rituals through Cass and Julia's courtship is rather like leafing through an album of old brown snapshots—the breathless discovery of shared affection, the arrival at an "understanding," the whispered secret, the joshing of friends, the solemn burial of previous courtships, anxiety about the other person's mother, eager expressions of mutual unworthiness, the taut ceremony of engagement, the treasured diamond, a crisis or two to test the other's firm intentions, careful caresses by parlor gaslight, imagining one's wedding. This expected rhythm for approaching marriage survived only in fragments a century later. In the 1880s its viability was intact, implicitly governing the performance of middle-class young folks seeking out their mates.[2]

Julia showed her conformity to ritual—and her poise—soon after she and Cass rediscovered one another by traveling from Lake Minnetonka to meet his mother in St. Paul. Early exchanges between the two women were pleasant but cool, and this tone lasted through most of the courtship. If Cass was bent on falling in love, it appeared that his mother decided to approve the choice and tried hard not to think about losing her son to another woman. In fact, she outdid herself in staging an engagement dinner for the couple at her Ashland Avenue home in St. Paul in November 1886, on Cass's twenty-seventh birthday. It was the first time she had invited guests to the house in over two years. The dinner was catered, an elaborate thirteen-course display—raw oysters, red snapper, beef filet, sweetbreads, breast of partridge, cheese soufflé, all graced with sweetened ices and concluding in a flourish of brandied peaches, bonbons, salted almonds, and coffee (but no wine or liquor)—served by two black waiters in swallow tail coats and white gloves.

After dinner Julia displayed her diamond in the parlor. Three days later she wrote from Milwaukee: "The gas has just been lighted and I am watching my ring sparkle and send forth happy bright colors in the light. Do you not want to say good evening to it?" But she returned to St. Paul only once more before their wedding a year later. Cass's mother was one reason. The tight bond between mother and son, and the threat that she seemed to pose to it, bothered Julia. "There is no earthly reason why Mrs. Gilbert should like me," she told Cass. "Just suppose that the more she sees of me the less she would like me. I assure you it makes me quite unhappy to think of it." Throughout their courtship Cass acted as a nervous liaison between the two women, torn between them, hoping for the best.[3]

That was not the only strain. Though Cass broke free to visit Milwaukee as often as his work allowed, theirs was mainly a courtship by correspondence. They wrote letters to each other two or three times a week for over a year, often chasing mail wagons to the train station after dark, spending extra for special delivery, and fretting about letters that crossed in the night. Long-distance telephones lay years ahead. "[No] one who had to depend on the railroad for their love would ever call that road smooth," Julia mused after a few weeks of it. For his part, Cass joked that he had "forsaken Architecture to write love letters."[4]

Julia turned out to be a gifted and fetching lover by mail. She promised that her letters would teach Cass "all the little traps and managements that girls make use of." "We are a dreadful set," she added confidently, "but very interesting to study nevertheless." She then proceeded to entice him with sensuous fancies that seem more torrid today than they were in the 1880s, when premarital sex among urban middle-class couples was rarely attempted and more rarely achieved. Her coquetry, protected by distance and prevailing rules, was downright seductive.

Six weeks into the courtship: "Oh Cass Cass I wish you were with me this instant. I long to tease you, there is nothing I would not do this morning." Christmas 1886, when sickness delayed Cass's visit to Milwaukee: "We will have a delightful quiet time together and I will show you what an irresistable nurse I can make." March 1887: "So here I am, saying in my most persuasive tones, 'Julie wants to be loved please.' I am thinking, even while I write, that you are sitting here beside me, and I am laughing at you and singing to you, and now I have stopped in the middle of my song because, well because, I like better just now to be made love to rather than sing." Six weeks before their wedding, a dream of married life, sitting before the fire: "And after we have been still for a long time I shall go quietly over to your chair and lean over it and kiss you, and then you will have to love me until it is time to light the gas."[5]

Cass lacked the talent to match this imagery. Mainly he responded with lunging desires to come to Milwaukee to hug her and then store up her kisses in the mail.

The reality beneath these romantic sallies was that Cass and Julia did not know each other very well. They both worried a bit about that. Less than a month into their courtship Julie wondered, "Do you think God made us for one another and so, since his works are always in harmony, there was no need of our knowing each other so intimately before?" And a little later, "My blessed Cass, you make me tremble. I am probably the most commonplace young woman of your acquaintance, and I dread the time when a more prolonged inspection of my merits and demerits will convince you of the fact." Cass promptly assured her that if she were too perfect he would not have a ghost of a chance with her, given his own flaws—about which, however, he could not bring himself to be very specific.[6]

When Julia invited him to join her for Communion next time he visited, it was Cass's turn for a serious display of self-doubt. He was not ready for Communion:

> I have allowed myself to be so completely engrossed in the affairs of the present and in an ambition for a certain kind of success, that almost all my old feelings of a personal interest in the Bible as a guide to a good life have been gradually smothered. . . . I do not disbelieve, I do not seriously question, but the discouraging thing is that I am content to let the whole matter go, my mind is full of other things, and they clog it. . . . I want to be right [but] I go about it in a perfunctory way, genuine in my intention, but soon forgetful. My heart is not in it, and I doubt my sincerity.

Julia pounced on this. It was not a matter of being good enough to take Communion, she lectured him. Christ died to forgive their sins, she explained: "*Because* we are sinners we ought to go to Communion." She then cited chapter and verse of Paul's epistle to the Romans for Cass to study. Cass thanked her for the lesson and meekly promised that when they were married he would help her keep a Christian home.[7]

The thickest thread in their correspondence had to do with architecture. Cass was bent on making sure that Julia understood its importance for him. Falling in love, he told her early on, had rejuvenated his career: "I have again that old pure feeling about my work, and the desire to do it well for its own sake and because I love it, and it is part of my life, and I was made to do it and for nothing else." This was Julia's first written warning about the engine of ambition she had decided to marry.[8]

He wanted her to know with precision how avidly he pursued his work and so described a typical day to her. The report has value for its glimpse into a young architect's routine a long century ago, as well as for its evidence of his insistence on personal control over his work. Cass was up and off at 7:30 A.M., like a physician making his rounds. He first stopped at the nearby Presbyterian church being built on Dayton Avenue, to check progress and correct some flaws:

> My word is law; and if it is not up to the mark down it comes no matter what it costs to make it right . . . Sometimes I find the material delivered is defective, and the defect has been skilfully concealed. A sharp reprimand follows . . . There is a row imminent, and no end of trouble on hand, but a firm word or two and then a pleasant one avoids the row and attains the end . . . Then with the carpenter a moment to test the strength of the beams . . . A word with the man who is waiting to ask about some iron work, a hasty explanation of a drawing to one of the mechanics, a smile and a pleasant word to a laborer as he passes (for nothing gets one better service than a kind word . . . to one whose life must be a dull monotony of toil) . . . Away I go to the next place. This is where an honest Swede is digging for a foundation. A little inspection of his lines and the location stakes shows he is getting on all right . . . He is working down in the pit with his men and teams, doing two days work in one . . . I rush off to meet Mrs. Bigelow about some decorations. This is in the quiet of an occupied house. A little talk, a reference to the principles of good taste, a discussion of some recent magazine article, a few practical suggestions, and the thing is settled . . . Next to the office . . . Dr. Bryant has been in, wants to know if his plans are nearly ready. Mr. Warren comes in tearing his hair because his estimates were $500 higher than anybody expected. Then a beggar, a match boy, a tramp, a peddlar, and a capitalist in succession. Mrs. Noyes wants to know if I can meet her at the office at four o'clock . . . The afternoon is spent in my office, seeing people, writing letters arranging business, making a sketch for this thing or a de-

> sign for that, calculating weights on a pier, or the strains on a wall, talking with a foundry man about an iron roof truss, making a water color sketch for a summer cottage.[9]

Cass decided further that Julia needed careful tutoring in what lay behind it all. He told her to read the discourses of the French theorist Viollet le Duc, whose wisdom he had absorbed at MIT. A little later he added Charles Eliot Norton on medieval churches to her required list. When his hero H. H. Richardson died that fall, he urged her to read Henry Van Brunt's tribute to him in the *Atlantic Monthly*. "There is so much in it that exactly coincides with my own ideas," he added rather ponderously, "that I may be able in that way to explain in a measure my own attitude toward my profession in regard to its higher aim."

Julia responded to all this with lighthearted bravery. "I have commenced my studies in architecture," she reported. "But after trying to imagine an ancient temple in which I placed the architrave on the floor, reared nine Doric pillars above, and surmounted the whole by a caryatid, I have come to the conclusion that my Saturday reading will have to be done over again." Cass then confided to her his tactics for landing commissions and, in anticipation of their future together, began to tap her practical savvy. "I don't believe it is 'the thing' for a man to look to his wife for advice on business matters," he wrote, "but when we are married that is precisely what I am going to do. Because you have clear insight and good judgment."[10]

Julia's musical talent also impressed Cass. He cheerfully acknowledged that his own understanding of music was confined to conventional preferences and asked her to repair his technical ignorance. But he could not resist trying out some architectural metaphors on her. Beethoven conjured for him early Romanesque cathedrals. Mozart's "infinite delicacy and fancy," he wrote, "seem to me like the beautiful lacework tracery of some rare old Gothic window." About Wagnerian opera: "great, splendid somber piles, whose strong lines and broad surfaces, deep mysterious shadows, and stately masses are sublime." Julia's response to these efforts was delightfully polite: "Your idea of music is very good, dear, and I am sure the more you know of it the more you will love it." For her part, she promised, she fully intended to finish Viollet le Duc's *Discourses* some day in the very near future.[11]

Three weeks into his engagement, Cass received a long letter from Joseph Wells, his irreverent bachelor friend at 57 Broadway, warning him not to get married. "In France," Wells wrote, "they have a proverbial expression 'He got married' to explain a failure." He proceeded to cite several famous authorities to nail down the point that marriage would be the ruination of Gilbert's life as artist and architect. "Be sure to remember," he concluded, "that no matter how calmly it is entered into, or how late in life, marriage is always done in a desperate hurry, and that I have Beethoven, Shakespeare, Michelangelo, Plato, and all philosophers and great men on my side while you have only the Almighty on yours." Cass laughed the letter off as a fresh sample of Wells's sardonic humor. But his mother took offense when he showed it to her, so he decided not to let Julia read it until after they were married and she had met Wells. "I don't want to run the risk of your disliking one of my best friends," he told her.[12]

Wells had touched a nerve, however. As the months of their engagement passed, and Julia's letters came to dwell on wedding plans, the nuances of social diplomacy toward friends and relatives, and the niche she wanted "in society," Cass seems to have felt an occasional twinge of nostalgia for the more spacious life he had once known as a free and urbane artist in Paris and Manhattan. A business trip to New York in May 1887 brought back to him the quick pulse of the place. He wrote to Julia about calling on friends at the Dakota, dining at Delmonico's, happily debating with Wells and Stanford White the merits of White's ornamental chair for Saint-Gaudens's standing Lincoln in Chicago, joining in a brisk critique of John LaFarge ("while he is the greatest colorist of our times he is the least to be relied upon"), sharing a lavish dinner with the Whites, and two good hours with William Mead and his interesting new wife—"a Hungarian with olive complexion, soft brown hair and gray eyes." The cosmopolitan lure of Manhattan was manifest.[13]

A month later, back in St. Paul and in a radically different mood, Cass told Julia how he felt about his artistry, in language that implicitly excluded her. He confessed to a familiar "queer feeling when I am doing imaginative work." He put his life into his art but he knew that no one else could quite understand how he felt about it. "And I feel that I am working for nothing at all, to no purpose, with no result. . . . I don't know what I want. I don't know how I would have it different. But I feel starved and lonesome for that intelligent sympathetic atmosphere of congenial friends that we used to think were around us in the days in New York." Then he told Julia about meeting an old friend from his days in the Latin Quarter in Paris, a fellow whose peculiar manner and appearance Gilbert chalked up to his being an artist. "I like to know such men, they are more near the real natural human being than some of our very correctly dressed and formal mannered friends who are apt to be just a trifle artificial." Cass concluded, "I am afraid that after we are married I will worry you a good deal by inviting my old bohemian friends from time to time."[14]

Julia's letters never responded to these wayward impulses. She remained much more concerned about Cass's mother than about his bohemian friends. Concern turned to alarm when Cass wrote that his mother wanted them to move into her St. Paul house after their marriage and when he later proposed to design "a double house for Mother and us." Julia mulled over these prospects and wondered if their marriage should not be postponed until they could afford a house of their own, where they might start life together without a hovering mother-in-law.[15]

She responded more cheerfully when Cass began touting the merits of apartment living, the latest modern arrangement among young couples. He located a new St. Paul apartment for them, the Albion at Selby and Western Avenue, in early summer 1887. The advantages were clear. Cass rattled them off from his viewpoint: elevators, dumbwaiters, no furnace work or lawn work or sidewalks to shovel, no tramps or peddlers or live-in servants to worry about. For her part Julia found very appealing the prospect of light housekeeping and regular meals with friends at the attached cafe—a common feature of the new apartment living in the 1880s. Like many young women of her family status she didn't know much about cooking or cleaning. "Life is not worth living without servants," she told Cass, but she was ready to try it for a while. She even decided to practice a bit. "I have swept!" she soon announced in triumph. "It was not such a dreadful undertaking after all. The sweeping I do not mind at all, but the dusting!! When we get into our apartment I am going to open all the windows and let the wind blow through the rooms and thus *blow* the dust out." Letters back and forth about furnishing and decorating the apartment pulled Cass and Julia closer. "Of course everything we have will have to be simple," Cass wrote, "but then that's no reason why it should not be in good taste." He told her essentially the same thing about their wedding ceremony.[16]

As the wedding approached, their engagement took on aspects of a roller coaster. A brief visit by Julia to St. Paul in early summer 1887 had not helped. Mrs. Gilbert's frosty manner startled Julia and discouraged Cass from talking through their wedding plans together with his mother. Julia vacationed by herself in Wisconsin later that summer, sailing, fishing, playing tennis, and worrying happily about acquiring too deep a suntan. Cass meanwhile occasionally left work for some rowing on the Mississippi. He also took in a couple of St. Paul Saints baseball games with Jim Taylor, yelling and cheering and tossing coins out at their favorite players. In August he spent a weekend hunting in the northern Minnesota lake country. Julia was happy to learn that he could relax, and asked if he would take her hunting too some day. "I feel perfectly confident that I should not scream every time you fired," she promised, "and there is just a possibility that I might shoot something myself—by mistake."[17]

Then a sudden September storm gusted through their romance. A passing query from Cass about her wanting to marry an overworked architect set Julia off: "Cass, don't you want to marry me? If you don't, tell me so, but do not keep me so uncertain and anxious any more, it is killing me. I cannot stand it." If he didn't want her, she would take a job offer at Elmira College in upstate New York teaching music instead. The needed assurances from Cass arrived by return mail, and the September crisis subsided swiftly. Within a week she was daydreaming by mail about married life—waiting for Cass to come home from work for her kiss, and "when you are particularly preoccupied I will devote myself to my books and music till the maid announces dinner." Cass's heavy work schedule did provoke a tart letter from her soon after that: "Are you going to be able to get away to be married, please? . . . One thing I do beg, let us finish getting married when we once commence, it would be so difficult to remember just where we left off."[18]

Their romance endured one last ripping disruption, twelve days before marriage. When Cass finally brought himself to spell out their wedding plans for his mother, she broke down in tears. Through the sobs came her reaction: her beloved Cass, having left her in ignorance so long about their plans, was now withdrawing his affection from her. Therefore she could not be present at the ceremony. Cass was flattened. His mother, he explained to Julia, remained the most important person in his life. "No one can know what we have been to one another," he wrote. "She has lavished on me all her love and pride and ambition. I have been her favorite son . . . and now she tells me I am leaving her. No one can take her place in my heart, Julie, for it is a peculiar one, and my love for my wife can not be less strong or pure because of the love I shall always have for my Mother." Cass felt helpless, torn between two demanding women. Only Julia could mend the conflict. "She seemed to think you were taking me from her," he wrote. "She wants your love, Julie, she wants a daughter's comforting sympathy. Your kind heart will tell you how best to offer it. . . . [At] the first advance you will have won for yourself the love of the strongest, noblest, most unselfish heart that ever beat. . . . Write to her at once. . . ." Thus responsibility for solving the mother problem in St. Paul passed to the sweetheart in Milwaukee.[19]

Julia met the challenge. The letter she wrote to Mrs. Gilbert worked, and she soon received from St. Paul a pretty swatch of lace to perfect her wedding dress. But her letter back to Cass prickled with quiet reproof. She asked if he had by now managed to discuss with his mother the wedding plans they had agreed on. "I think it would have been better last summer, dear, if you had encouraged my talking over things with her instead of fearing that she would not understand me nor like me," she wrote. Then this: "I think it will always be best for me to manage my friends in my own way." Next she asked Cass to buy her a new wedding ring, instead of using his father's ring to marry her. She was sure it would make his mother happier if Cass himself wore his father's ring. Julia went on to specify that her own new ring be made with square edges, not rounded. "I believe," she said, "in meeting this world and things in general squarely." All this struck home as intended. Cass finally took full blame for the whole misunderstanding and pleaded with Julia to accept his father's ring. She had made her point and thus finally agreed.[20]

The wedding, a "quiet wedding" in the parlance of the day, took place as planned in the parlor of Julia's uncle's home in Milwaukee on November 29, 1887. Cass and his bride then left for a ten-day wedding trip to New York City. On the same day Cass's mother, conspicuous in her absence from the ceremony, closed her house in St. Paul and headed west to live with her eldest son, Charlie, in Southern California. The mother and her favorite son shared a last exchange of sentiments. She told Cass that he had left her desolated by going off to start a home of his own without her. She hoped he would nevertheless eventually remember that "your home is where your Mother is." For his part Cass wrote more cryptically: "I do not feel that I am going out of the home, Mother, except for just a little while and then we will be together again." Neither letter mentioned Julia Finch.[21]

But Julia emerged the clear winner. She had survived the long contest for Cass Gilbert's devotion and replaced his mother as the strongest person in his life. Moreover, by marrying Cass she went far to resolve the conflict that long roiled inside him, between the dreamy artist recalling his taste of bohemia and the ambitious architect yearning to succeed. The home and family Julia prepared for Cass would soon banish bohemia from their table. Instead they now headed together for respectable success.

Durham Cathedral, England, watercolor, Cass Gilbert, 1913.
(Smithsonian American Art Museum, bequest of Emily Finch Gilbert through Julia Post Bastedo, executor)

Latin Quarter, Paris, France, watercolor and pencil, Cass Gilbert, 1880.
(Smithsonian American Art Museum, bequest of Emily Finch Gilbert through Julia Post Bastedo, executor)

Virginia Avenue (sic, *actually Ashland Avenue) House for Elizabeth Wheeler Gilbert, St. Paul, wash on gray paper, Cass Gilbert, 1882–84.*

(Negative number 69636T, © Collection of The New-York Historical Society)

Dayton Avenue Presbyterian Church, St. Paul, elevation sketch, Gilbert and Taylor, 1886.
(Negative number 71480T, © Collection of The New-York Historical Society)

Detail, Battle of Nashville, *Howard Pyle, Governor's Reception Room, Minnesota State Capitol.*
(Photo by author)

Quadriga, Daniel Chester French, Minnesota State Capitol.
(Photo by author)

Interior dome, Minnesota State Capitol.
(Photo by Eric Mortenson, MHS Collections)

Senate chamber, Minnesota State Capitol.
(Photo by Eric Mortenson, MHS Collections)

Exterior, Minnesota State Capitol.
(Photo by Eric Mortenson, MHS Collections)

7

Hard Times

During their first seven years of marriage, Julia gave birth to four children—three daughters (Emily, Elizabeth, and Julia) and then a son, Cass, Jr., who became his father's heir apparent the day he was born. Cass turned out to be an avid and adoring father when he had time. He enjoyed reading stories to his children, and when he was on the road he wrote long letters about things he witnessed or imagined, often illustrated with elaborate sketches. In their early years, when his children might not be expected to fully understand what he described, his correspondence carried instructions that letters be saved for future contemplation.

Cass was on the road a lot, monitoring residential jobs beyond St. Paul and searching for larger institutional commissions to improve his reputation and his income. If anything, marriage deepened his commitment to his calling. Six months after his wedding he wrote, "To become an Architect in the right sense of the word means that a man shall give his life to it and nothing else, and shall study the work he has to do with enthusiastic interest in every detail pertaining to it, and content himself with nothing less than complete success."[1]

Complete success remained elusive. Cass scrambled hard for fresh work, hoping to lift his yearly income to $2,000, the level he felt necessary to lead a respectable married life. He told Julia that "sometimes I am afraid you will ask what becomes of the artist when he thinks so much of money-getting." Over the next few years he lived with the elemental fact that his artistry depended on landing jobs. Money-getting was on his mind when he entered the competition for a large state hospital in St. Paul, his first venture into the politics of public architecture. He thought the commission was tilting his way, and he was about to head east to study hospital design, when a rival contestant applied his political leverage and the job slipped away. Cass told Julia that he and his partner, Jim Taylor, had been "unwilling to compromise our position or lower our professional standard by appealing to 'influence' for influence sake alone." Cass clearly lacked experience in this field, but he was a fast and flexible learner.[2]

He next competed for the design of the New York Life Insurance Company's ten-story downtown office building in St. Paul. Again he lost. But it happened that Daniel Willard, a partner in the New York architectural firm that won the commission, was an old friend from their days together at MIT and then at McKim, Mead and White. When Willard visited St. Paul to inspect the building site, Cass gave him a tour of his own buildings in the city and told him that he and Taylor were "not only the *best* but the *only* men who could conduct the work for him." Then he accompanied Willard back to New York, hoping to clinch a deal with Willard's partners to superintend their St. Paul project. "This is all great fun," he told Julia. "It is like hunting large game and there is lots of excitement about it, while at the same time one must seem entirely cool and to a large extent disinterested." This time Cass's tactics worked. He landed his big job for the year ahead and told Julia that he now hoped to design and build a house for her even before their apartment lease ran out.[3]

The New York Life Insurance high-rise underwent several design changes during Gilbert's superintendence. He also found himself mediating violent strife between the Swedish and Irish immigrants in the construction crew. The building was finally completed in 1889. Soon thereafter a large bronze American eagle, a company symbol sculpted by Augustus Saint-Gaudens, went up over the main entry. When the building came down eighty years later, preservationists saved Saint-Gaudens's eagle from the demolition and moved it to a new location in downtown St. Paul, near the Endicott Building on Fourth Street.[4]

Endicott-on-Fourth Building, 143-145 East Fourth Street, St. Paul, 1890.
(MHS Collections)

The Endicott Building itself is regarded today as one of the city's finer architectural landmarks. It was Cass Gilbert's first commercial triumph. His success in winning the commission for it in 1889 marked a decisive breakthrough in his young career. Beyond that, the story behind the Endicott Building is also part of a larger historical drama that deeply affected Gilbert's subsequent fortunes.

The drama began with a flood of investment capital into the Midwest from the Atlantic seaboard and from Europe toward the end of the nineteenth century. The broad flow of this money, the strong knots of corporate power it subsidized, and its sudden ebbing in the early 1890s made for one of the most turbulent chapters in American economic history, one that ended in the worst depression of the nineteenth century.

Boom, followed by bust, brought with it political repercussions that transformed the nation's labor market. These included the outbreak of wage-worker insurgency that swelled and then flattened the ranks of the legendary Knights of Labor and the emergence after that of a tough and viable new trade union movement under the leadership of Samuel Gompers. The same years witnessed the rise and fall of Midwestern agrarian Granger protest against arbitrary rail rates; the messianic appeal of Henry George's Single Tax crusade against absentee land ownership; and the angry Populist thrust of the People's Party, the most radical and prophetic third-party reform movement in American history.

Out of this turmoil emerged a national two-party realignment, which has endured more or less to the present day. This has pitted a relatively liberal Democratic Party, which ultimately adopted much of the Populist and trade union agenda, against a relatively conservative Republican Party, which largely absorbed the energies of business expansionism and the anxious moral values of its middle-class supporters. The public policy realignment of the 1890s would mark a decisive watershed in the fortunes of millions of Americans, famous and obscure. It would structure Cass Gilbert's political thought and behavior for the rest of his life, as his early Republican Party inclinations matured into a personal act of faith.

Of course Cass could not know what rocky times lay just ahead for him as he maneuvered to win the trust and friendship of eastern investors like William and Henry Endicott in the Twin Cities boom of the 1880s. To him, the Endicotts represented the best of their breed—two gentlemanly Boston entrepreneurs in imported dry goods, railroads, and real estate who were interested in the prospects for profits in fast-growing areas out west such as St. Paul. The Endicott brothers were direct descendents of John Endecott [*sic*], the first governor of the Massachusetts Bay colony in the early seventeenth century. More recently William Endicott had helped to found both the Republican Party and the Massachusetts Institute of Technology. Cass Gilbert and others assumed that this type of financier's economic impact on St. Paul could hardly be more benign. In June 1888 negotiations got underway between the Endicott brothers and Gilbert and Taylor for a new office building in the heart of St. Paul's prospering business district. Cass went to Boston to interview the Endicotts, dine with them at the venerable Tavern Club (an event he described in detail for daughter Emily to read about some day), and hammer out plans for the building. These called for a six-story structure, equipped with the latest elevator and sanitation technology, with an L-shaped footprint wrapping around the taller Pioneer Press Building which had recently gone up on the prominent downtown corner of Fourth and Robert Streets. An alluring arcade of retail shops would connect the two legs of the Endicott surrounding the Pioneer.[5]

This was Cass's first chance to build big for rich clients, and he made the most of it. He wanted to create a structure whose grace, dignity, and disciplined detailing would set it apart from the exuberant complexities of its neighbors. He called it his "chef d'oeuvre" and told his mother that "the style is so pure and so simple and so carefully carried out that it will be considered a scholarly piece of work."[6]

The building's exterior, finished in red sandstone and pressed brick, was influenced, as he later noted, by the Villard mansions on Madison Avenue in New York, the McKim, Mead and White commission for which his friend Joseph Wells had fashioned the Italian Renaissance refinements. For the main entry to the Endicott Building, however, Cass designed a robust rounded archway, which recalled the signature entries of his hero H. H. Richardson. Wells was quick to censure this detail. When Cass sent photos of the building to New York for his approval, Wells found the entry conformed "too much to the Richardsonian order of things to harmonize with any style of architecture requiring good proportion,"—a value that was, in his opinion, "apparently not even suspected by Henry Hobson Richardson and his imitators." Well aware of Gilbert's veneration of Richardson, Wells went on to belittle the master: "No matter how clever or great the individual architect may be, no matter how sublime the personality, or how successful in bullying committees and clients, these qualities can never make an outlandish thing handsome." Otherwise, Wells acknowledged, "the general effect [of the Endicott] is *very good*, and dignified." He decided that Gilbert on balance merited his congratulations.[7]

Endicott Building interior arcade.
(MHS Collections)

Wells's critique must have stung. Cass sent his rebuttal not to Wells but to his own mother, assuring her that the Endicott "will be generally considered one of the fine things in this country." He stressed the "delicate and graceful" proportions of the main entry that Wells had deprecated. "I hope Mother that you will like it and be proud of it. If you are, I shall not care who don't like it." He need not have worried. Architect Frank Bacon wrote from Boston asking for a photo of the Endicott's main façade: "I want it. I've been bragging about it to the fellows here!" Thomas Hastings of the New York firm Carrere and Hastings wrote to say, "I shall always look forward with great interest for your work and count upon you to awaken them in the west." Best of all was an unexpected letter from Chicago's Daniel Burnham, who had paused while passing through St. Paul to report of "the pleasure your Endicott Building gave me, when seeing it this morning." Both plan and exterior seemed "manly," "well studied," and "satisfactory," Burnham added. This praise from the West's most celebrated architect must have brought a glow to Gilbert and his office staff.[8]

Eastern press opinion was also heartening, not least for its discovery that elegance was possible out on the upper Mississippi. Commentators in New York and Boston had long been in the habit of referring to "western vernacular" architecture and regretting what they called its brash, undisciplined appearance. Gilbert's Endicott building clearly countered this condescension. An effusive writer in *Cosmopolitan* called its arcade of imported marbles and opalescent glass a small "metropolis in itself," designed by "one of the Saintly City's talented young architects"—right there in the middle of the "wild and woolly west." Montgomery Schuyler wrote more authoritatively in *Harper's*: "So ostentatiously discreet is the detail of this building, indeed, so minute the scale of it, and so studious the avoidance of anything like stress," that it seemed like a quiet remonstrance against the "westerness" surrounding it.[9]

The same year Gilbert landed the Endicott commission, 1888, he also won the chance to design an apartment complex called Portland Terrace—another first in his young career—located a short block off

RICHARDSONIAN ENTRY PORCHES

(right)
Portland Terrace, off Summit Avenue, St. Paul, Cass Gilbert, 1888.

(facing page, top)
Trinity Church rectory, Boston, H. H. Richardson, 1880.

(facing page, bottom)
John and Frances Glessner House, Chicago, H. H. Richardson, 1886.
(Photos by author)

Summit Avenue in St. Paul. A hip-roofed red brick building with an I-shaped ground plan, Portland Terrace is distinguished at its western end by a round-arched entryway, which recalls in simplified form Richardsonian entry porches, including the Trinity Church Rectory (1880) in Boston and the Glessner House (1886) in Chicago. (Richardson's entry porch designs, with a masonry porch barrier extending halfway in from one base of the arch framing the recess, evidently appealed to another young architect then launching his career, Frank Lloyd Wright. Long fascinated by circular entry arches, Wright employed the Richardsonian porch detail as late as 1947 for his entry to the V. C. Morris Shop in San Francisco.)

When Portland Terrace was completed, Cass and Julia rented one of its apartment units briefly, until the birth of their first child in 1889, which inspired Cass to begin fashioning a home of their own. He chose an attractive site along the bluff below Summit Avenue looking out toward the Mississippi. The house itself, which survives considerably altered on Heather Place, is a modest structure compared

with those he designed nearby for more wealthy clients. In some ways its boxy compaction anticipates the northern adaptation of the bungalow so popular with a coming generation. But its textured surfaces of warm red sandstone blocks below shingled gables, rising to a gambrel roofline interrupted by dormers and an open porch, also captured the earlier mood of the Shingle Style, picturesque and cozy. The uncluttered simplicity in the finish of interior spaces, free from the fuss of Victorian adornment, reflected Cass's tight budget as well as the moderating influence of his favorite novelist William Dean Howells. And his admiration for the quiet efficiency of his modern flush toilet led him to lavish praise on its Philadelphia manufacturer. He boasted so cheerfully about the whole achievement that one of his old architectural lunch partners in New York shot back in jest, "I've been hoping to receive a photograph or two of your house just to see what crimes you can commit when you are not restrained by the sober good sense of [an] intelligent client."[10]

Cass Gilbert House, 1 Heather Place, St. Paul, ca. 1890.
(Photo by author)

That was the last note of jocularity in Gilbert's career for several more years. In fall 1890, his new house not yet fully completed, he and Jim Taylor felt a sickening business slump as the western construction boom of the 1880s tailed off. Owing to several months' delay in clients' payments for completed work, Gilbert and Taylor fell behind in rental payments on their own office. Over previous years Cass and his mother and brothers had gathered good profits from family rental properties in St. Paul. Now these began to tumble, too. Cass sought a way out of the collapse through a desperate search for political patronage. When he learned that plans were afoot in Washington for a new federal office complex in St. Paul, combining post office, courthouse, and custom house, he applied to President Benjamin Harrison's secretary of the treasury, William Windom, for the post of construction superintendent for the project. Windom, Minnesota's senior Republican politician, had provided letters of introduction for Cass's European tour a decade before. Now in 1890 Cass

Cass Gilbert House interior.
(MHS Collections)

asked for help again. While assuring Windom that he did not propose to base his application entirely "upon political grounds," Cass fortified it with over a dozen letters of support from Minnesota congressmen, senators, and former governors. Railroader James J. Hill also pitched in his influence. The campaign succeeded. Over the next two years Cass drew eight dollars a day from this federal patronage post. His involvement in the building project was confined to supervising the basement excavation, a task barely completed when Grover Cleveland's 1893 return to the White House terminated Cass in favor of a Democrat. His dismissal, like his original appointment, was fresh proof that the spoils system still governed the politics of public architecture.[11]

Construction of the building got underway a year later but was not completed until 1904. A soaring hybrid designed by Chicago architect Willoughby Edbrooke, it survives recycled as St. Paul's Landmark Center. Gilbert had hardly anything to do with its construction or appearance.

Cass fought for a real job throughout the economic slump. First he tried to activate his old connection with McKim, Mead and White, offering to supervise the firm's work for the upcoming Chicago World's Fair. His St. Paul practice was at a standstill, he confessed to William Mead, with no prospect of better times soon. He was free to move. "Why don't you abandon the West," Mead replied, "and settle in New York or if you can stand it Chicago." Mead noted that all the work for the fair was in the hands of Chicago's Daniel Burnham.[12]

Days later in January 1891 Burnham's beloved partner John Wellborn Root died. Mead promptly began promoting Gilbert to replace him. Burnham was a great organizer, Mead told Cass, but he needed a first-rate designer. At Gilbert's request Mead broached the idea with Burnham, and Burnham was open to it. What little he had seen of Gilbert's work had impressed him. He added, however, that "John's death has left a hole into which not one, but several strong men must be flung, to even approximately level it up again." Cass may have bristled at this sentiment. When he went to Chicago to present his case directly to Burnham, friction soon surfaced. Cass had already made clear that a two-man partnership was what he had in mind. After looking over Burnham's Chicago operation, he spelled out his proposal in detail: two years as Burnham's salaried associate, followed if all went well by a full partnership, with Gilbert's share of the firm's proceeds rising steadily toward 50–50.

Now it was Burnham's turn to bristle. He and Gilbert were comparative strangers, he noted, and might not prove to be congenial. He wanted no talk about a partnership until "we have been long enough in harness together for me to know you, and what is more important for you to know me and feel sure you would like to live with me." He offered Cass an office salary for two years, plus whatever profits his independent work brought in, this work to be carried out under Gilbert's name alone. Cass found this offer both "obscure" and "offensive," and in another somewhat frosty Chicago meeting he talked Burnham into accepting his previous terms. He went home thinking he had maneuvered Chicago's pre-eminent architect into a firm deal. He should have known better. To his dismay Burnham soon informed him by mail that complications had arisen and the proposal must be dropped. Less than a month later Charles Atwood entered Burnham's office as Root's successor in building design, on the recommendation of William R. Ware, Gilbert's old mentor at MIT. Atwood had once apprenticed under Ware and enjoyed a brilliant reputation as a neoclassicist among those who knew him. What else Cass knew about him was not all that flattering in his mind.[13]

What had happened baffled Cass. His negotiations with Burnham, which he called "the crisis of my professional career," had turned into a contest in which he managed to lose the job by winning the debate over it. Young, proud, and starchy, he may have struck Burnham, who was a somewhat imperious man accustomed to easy command, as not quite worth the trouble. Other personality differences doubtless figured in. Burnham, like Root and so many other giants of those days—Richardson, Saint-Gaudens, Stanford White—enjoyed a hearty, sensual, earthy living style. Through each of them, in the phrase of a contemporary who knew them all well, "ran the pagan strain characteristic of the artist . . . they had none of the austerity of the Puritan." Atwood turned out to fit the pagan type all too well. Rumors floated that he took dope and had a secret wife somewhere in the east. He became the single most prolific designer in the creation of Chicago's White City of 1893, however, winning six prizes for his Chicago buildings, and he proved a valuable addition to Burnham's staff in other ways while he lasted. He died young, four years after joining Burnham.[14]

Cass was a manifestly different sort of fellow. In him were the makings of the last great Puritan in the country's architectural profession. He felt driven by status demands that guided American Puritan culture as it secularized itself across the nineteenth century. In the Darwinian mood of the post–Civil War era, struggling for survival to prove one's fitness supplanted the Puritan code of striving for salvation that Cass had absorbed as a Presbyterian youngster. The constant need to test himself against others continued to power the more assertive traits of his Puritan mentality. This was an aspect of Gilbert's nature that Burnham, a brusque but keen judge of men, doubtless noticed and decided to avoid.

Cass was also a buoyant young professional. He soon mastered whatever resentments he carried away from his bout with Burnham and afterwards rarely referred to what he called "the incident." His relations with Burnham remained carefully collegial if not exactly cordial. But he took a while to recover financially from the setback. His St. Paul practice remained so flat that in May 1891 he resorted to offering his talents to the editor of *Harper's Monthly* as an architectural illustrator. "The stagnation of business now prevailing makes it necessary for me to take some such step as this," he confessed. A month later he reached the grim but amicable decision with Jim Taylor to dissolve their partnership. The business simply was not there to hold the friends together. Taylor left St. Paul for Philadelphia in search of fresh possibilities, while Cass organized a new office in the Endicott Building, determined to work through the slump on his own. Overdue payments from old clients, combined with fierce competition for new commissions, made life at the office quite miserable at times. One day in October 1891 Cass vented exasperation over current conditions in his practice by composing a mock announcement from an imaginary client to architects at large:

> I propose to invite an unlimited competition among architects for the work proposed on my 3rd Street property. I to have the option of selecting any, or all, or none of the plans offered or to combine with the one selected such parts of the others as may suit my fancy, without compensation however to the architect or designer of same. I will pay two per cent commission to the successful competitor, payable ten years after completion of work . . .

Gilbert's point was clear. An environment of hard times severely weakened the architect in the grim balance of power between his job-hungry office and clients prepared to build. The experience hardened Gilbert's resolve to fortify the collective interest of architects through tighter professional organization and standards of practice.[15]

But all that awaited a brighter future. Cass found what he hoped was an antidote to his immediate problems in the personal patronage of the powerful railroader James J. Hill, whose acquaintance he had long cultivated as a fellow member of St. Paul's Minnesota Club. In the 1880s Hill had moved aggressively to build a rail empire in the Northwest that would overshadow and replace the troubled Northern Pacific. In 1889 he organized the Great Northern Railway Company, which controlled some 2,700 miles of track from Illinois to Montana. By 1893 the track reached Seattle. Hill remained a dedicated colonizer even after the frenzied western population boom of the early 1880s began to tail off. Without reliance on the lavish public subsidies enjoyed by earlier transcontinental lines, he was committed to building a functional economy of cities, towns, and farms along his western route and its many north-south spurs. For all his buccaneering tactics he was acknowledged to be the most effective rail tycoon of his age. Gilbert admired Hill's knack for success despite the adversity of both economic slumps and labor militancy. In summer 1891 he went to work designing rail depots for the millionaire.[16]

The Great Northern depot in Grand Forks, North Dakota, a local pocket of prosperity along the Red River, required Cass's personal oversight. A big rectangular stone structure in the Richardsonian manner, with stately clock tower and wraparound platform shed, his station—hailed at the time as Great Northern's finest between St. Paul and the Pacific—was complete by 1892.[17]

On each inspection trip to Grand Forks Cass was impressed by the growth he witnessed. The surrounding prairie, he recalled, "was staked out for streets and avenues and town lots, and real estate signs bloomed like the wild rose." The town itself possessed both a street railway and an opera house—two striking signals of urban vitality in the 1890s.

Elsewhere in the West things were different. Chronic drought and agrarian anger over eastern economic control were gathering support

Great Northern Depot, Grand Forks, North Dakota, 1892.
(MHS Collections)

for a host of radical reactions: Populism, currency inflation, and Henry George's Single Tax campaign to end poverty by abolishing absentee land ownership. George's radical reformism provoked Gilbert's special animosity. A single prohibitive tax on the unearned rental profits of parasitic landlords, George promised, would discourage land monopoly and enable working people to own their own homes on the land they worked. With the Single Tax in place, no further need would exist for the policies of government subsidy and regulation the Republican Party pursued in Washington to supervise national growth. A free economy of happy independent producers would flourish, and the millennium would be at hand.[18]

Both Henry George's arguments and his remedies angered Gilbert. He was personally vulnerable to George's indictment of absentee owners. He and his mother and brothers had been depending on rents from their real estate holdings in St. Paul now for over twenty years, creaming off income from tenants while scarcely lifting a finger to fix up the property. ("As to improving our old buildings," Cass once wrote to his brother Charles, "we have always felt that as long as we were getting a good rent anyway what was the use of improving. The location held the tenants and they could not afford to [move]." This was Henry George's exact point.) Moreover, as a young architect in search of big commissions, Cass believed implicitly in the excellence of western investments by absentee capitalists like Henry Villard and the Endicott brothers of Boston, as well as men like James J. Hill. Also by now Cass was a confirmed Republican, fully committed to the policies for promoting growth pursued by the Grand Old Party since the Civil War—policies that Henry George proposed to scrap.[19]

One night in September 1891 Cass spent an evening in his Grand Forks hotel room answering a letter from a New York City architect friend, John Beverly Robinson, who endorsed George's utopian crusade. Robinson's letter demanded refutation. Cass went at it with a passion, laying bare his own political beliefs with rare candor. All arguments about the unearned profits of rent were "very fallacious," he wrote, as was the Populist remedy of currency inflation for needy farmers. Absentee landownership was no problem so long as cheap land remained for western settlers to purchase. For just $12.50, a man could buy ten acres of North Dakota land, the finest in the world, and "even a newsboy can save that amount of money in a single year." After ten years of prudent farming he would be "absolutely independent" and would "care no more about 'rent and interest' than he cares where flies go in winter."

Cass also claimed that authentic distress in America was mainly confined to cities. Here he was invoking the conventional middle-class wisdom of the day. Distress should be remedied not by punishing the rich but "by sending the poor and oppressed to people the waste places of the earth and reap the fruits of honest independent labor until the desert shall bloom as the rose." (Roses seemed to bloom constantly on available cheap land in Gilbert's imagination.)

Most poor people clung to city life because they were "too lazy to make a living in the country, or too fond of the excitements and squalid pleasures of city life." Their minds must be enlarged by the lessons of "thrift, economy, and individual effort." Finally, Cass asserted his Republican conviction that the wealth of the rich did not hurt the poor. Much of that wealth wound up as wages in the pockets of working folk, and much of the rest enhanced society through "material improvements like railroads, steamship lines, public libraries, hospitals, and the thousand charities and benefits of civilization." In a nation where government policy fosters the creation of private wealth, and that wealth is wisely spent, those who for whatever reason remained in need could only benefit.[20]

Gilbert's angry response to Henry George's heresies exposed the heart of his own conservative beliefs. Typically, hard times breed radical dreams among working folk—dirt farmers and wage laborers—which only strengthen the contested faith of anxious middle-class social moralists, binding them more closely to established authority. So it was with Gilbert. Furthermore, he shared with most of his fellow architects a pervasive mistrust of labor militancy, which involved strikes and boycotts to win union recognition and the closed shop for carpenters, brick masons, plumbers, and rail workers. The collective demands of these craftsmen (inflamed, their critics believed, by mostly foreign-born agitators) could radically upset calculations about getting a job done on schedule at a decent profit. The lurching growth environment of the late nineteenth century inspired a strong implicit bias among architects, clients, and contractors against any obstacles thrown up by organized labor to delay more growth.[21]

Capitalist James J. Hill shared this outlook and would surely have endorsed the views of his embattled young architect. In fact, Gilbert's next big commission sprang directly from the tycoon's social agenda, which aimed to advance the work of the nation's leading liberal Catholic prelate, Archbishop John Ireland of St. Paul.

Archbishop Ireland believed in "Americanizing" the Roman Catholic population of the country, which was divided over the wisdom of parochial school separatism and the use of foreign languages in immigrant church services. Ireland opposed both these policies. Instead he promoted the colonization of the rural Northwest by assimilated, English-speaking Catholic immigrants. He was a Republican Party activist in an era when Irish Catholics were almost monolithic in their loyalty to the Democratic Party. He believed that the Church should foster the education of its own priesthood in America to counter the reactionary mood of the European hierarchy. His influence on each of these issues was so potent that one admirer called him the "consecrated blizzard of the Northwest."[22]

All that Ireland lacked was the money and domineering ways of James J. Hill to be Hill's clerical equivalent. Hill himself was a formidable personal force, rather primitive in appearance and awesome in manner—a shaggy-bearded gorilla of a man with one good eye and a barking voice who decorated his life with precious gems and metals, fine leather, and imported works of art. Hill's wife was a Roman Catholic, and she nurtured his sympathy for Catholic culture and the goal of Americanization. He also understood that the grip of the Church on its Catholic immigrant followers depended on a strong American-trained hierarchy and a thriving priesthood.

"Look at the millions of foreigners pouring into this country to whom the Roman Catholic Church represents the only authority that they either fear or respect," Hill once warned. He told his authorized biographer that philanthropic support for the educational efforts of men like Archbishop Ireland was "as much a matter of good business as is the improvement of farm stock or the construction of a faultless railroad bed." In 1891 he promised Archbishop Ireland a half million dollars to found a seminary for the training of American priests. The seminary's campus was to be located at the western end of Summit Avenue in St. Paul.[23]

Hill assigned the first six buildings for the St. Paul Seminary to Gilbert with a $200,000 budget ceiling. This lucrative commission soon engaged Cass in a triangular power struggle between Hill as patron, Ireland as client, and himself as architect. The struggle decisively advanced his education in architectural politics. After inspecting the seminary site with Ireland, Cass drew up preliminary sketches, which pleased the archbishop. But Hill, skeptical about Ireland's talents at cost control, and Gilbert's as well, reacted differently to Gilbert's sketches. He fixed his intimidating one-eyed glare on the young architect and told him that he was answerable to Hill, not the archbishop, on all issues touching design, construction, and cost. When Ireland and Gilbert called at Hill's new home on Summit Avenue (a vast, dour Romanesque pile designed by Peabody and Stearns of Boston) to present him with detailed plans for the seminary, Hill peremptorily rejected them.

"He denied, criticized or doubted every statement, estimate, remark, suggestion or figure that was placed before him," Cass fumed in his diary. "His manner and language was to the last degree exasperating, arrogant, and ungentlemanly. . . . I was disgusted with the whole performance, which was a mixture of conceit, egotism, and theatrical byplay (for effect upon Bishop Ireland and myself)."

When Cass went back the next night to argue his case, Hill pounded on over issues of cost. This ruffled Cass, and he stiffly replied that the tycoon need not worry about Gilbert's spending too much of his money. Then a strange thing happened. Hill said he had something to show Cass in his library. As Cass described it in his diary, the tycoon proceeded to unlock his library vault, pull out several handfuls of diamonds, opals, emeralds, and other jewels, and spread them across a table for Cass to contemplate. Hill chose this way to make clear to his architect that control, not cost, was the real point at issue between them. Psychologically abused by the jewels, Cass decided to leave Hill's mansion as quickly as possible. The next day Archbishop Ireland had to talk him out of dropping the seminary project on the spot.[24]

When negotiations resumed two months later, with Cass still badly in need of work, Hill's control was firmly established, and the project began to be called "the Hill Seminary." Hill told Cass to make the buildings as plain as factories, but, he added, "make them massive and something that will last and that we will not be ashamed of in five years." Two months after that a Gilbert office memo recorded, "Mr. Hill called in regard to drawings for Seminary. He said that they should have been sent down to his office for him to look over and see if [they] were correct. He said he doubted very much if they were. Also said that if you could not attend to this he must look for someone else." By this time Cass had hardened himself to the tycoon's insults and stayed with the job.

His buildings for the campus—dormitories, gymnasium, dining hall, administration and classroom space—were models of unembellished red-brick severity, appropriate for the lives of their users. Taken

Administration building, St. Paul Seminary, St. Paul, 1894.
(MHS Collections)

together, those that survive reach well beyond the ordinary in proportion and minimalist dignity. Campus construction had barely begun when the panic of 1893 rocked Hill's rail empire and halted the seminary project. When work resumed a year later, Archbishop Ireland deferred to Hill's decisions about furnishing the completed halls and even about the curriculum to be taught within. The power struggle between patron, client, and architect had turned out to be no contest. Gilbert despised the experience. Never again, he vowed, would he be coerced into subservience by a powerful client.[25]

The panic of 1893, harsher than any in history before the great crash of 1929, jolted Wall Street just as the Chicago World's Fair opened in the first week of May. The panic was a direct response to shrinking western growth and investors' fears about Populist-inspired currency inflation. Its impact on the city of Chicago was profound. It led to sudden soaring unemployment, the depression violence of the Pullman Strike a year later, and the conversion to Socialism of jailed strike leader Eugene Debs soon after that. But hard times in Chicago did not greatly diminish the avalanche of visitors—27 million of them—who passed through the city bound for the fairgrounds at Jackson Park, seven miles to the south along Lake Michigan.

The famous White City by the lake, commemorating 400 years since the Columbian voyage of discovery, rivals World War I as the most important event in American architectural history. The magnitude, stylistic harmony, and breathtaking visual impact of the fair's buildings and their magic landscape fixed the classical Beaux-Arts tradition at last in the American imagination as the defining essence of architectural rectitude and beauty. For most practitioners of Cass Gilbert's generation, as well as for Cass himself, it cleared the air of those aesthetic ambiguities that had been snarling the "battle of the styles" since the Civil War, and it opened space for the scenographic neoclassicism favored from then on by his generation. Forty years later Cass would recall that the White City "gave a glorious impulse to American architecture and was immensely beneficial." In 1893, however, the fair was yet another moment of disappointment for the struggling young architect. He was not nearly as caught up in it as he had hoped to be.[26]

Cass believed that if he had secured the partnership he sought from Daniel Burnham in 1891 he would have become designer-in-chief for the Chicago Fair instead of Charles Atwood, Burnham's final choice. Cass learned that Burnham's previous partner, John Wellborn Root, had just before his death drawn up a list of architects to be considered for major building assignments at the fair. Gilbert was on the list, and he was sure he would have been tapped if Root had lived. As it turned out, he was reduced to competing—unsuccessfully—for the design of the Minnesota Building at the fair. He was then named to a Jury of Architecture, a distinctly modest honor, charged with selecting examples of recent work around the country to be exhibited in photographs at the fair. The jury chose three entries submitted by Cass himself, to be hung with others in the main gallery of Charles Atwood's Palace of Fine Arts, the most celebrated of the several buildings Atwood designed for the fair. Cass visited the fairgrounds one afternoon while sitting with the jury in Chicago. He reported his terse approval in a letter home to Julia: "It is a grand, grand sight." But most of the letter was devoted to telling Julia about his chance meeting with the touring Polish pianist Paderewski in the bar of Louis Sullivan's Auditorium Hotel. Since Cass had no part in creating the White City, he did not revel much in its glories at the time.[27]

South façade of Fine Arts Building, World's Columbian Exposition, Chicago, 1893.
(Photo by C. D. Arnold, courtesy Chicago Historical Society)

The panic of 1893 hit Cass hard as it rumbled through the West. Eastern investments in western construction ventures evaporated, and banks in western cities began to fold. A bank in Milwaukee holding Cass's notes failed, and he spent the summer trying to bring his debts under control. His older brother Charlie in California also met trouble as he darted frantically from real estate to oil leases to sardine packing to avoid unemployment. When Cass sent him a bundle of used clothing, Charlie cheerfully complained that the pants were too big and accused Cass of approaching the proportions of a Grover Cleveland. Meanwhile, younger brother Sam lost his job in Chicago and also turned to Cass for help. When Cass again thought of leaving St. Paul for greener fields in the east, once more he was disappointed. Peabody and Stearns in Boston gave his overture a flat rebuff: "Probably we have no place good enough to offer you. I don't believe we have." At age thirty-five Cass must have wondered some days when and where it would end. "I am sorry to hear that you are 'busted,'" a friend wrote early in 1894, "Hope it will change soon." The birth of his son, Cass, Jr., later that spring must have added a keen edge of anxiety to Gilbert's calculations. But he had long since learned how to use adversity to test his own grit.[28]

In mid March 1894 he paid a visit to the St. Paul home of wholesale grocer Channing Seabury, an old Ashland Avenue neighbor of his mother. Seabury, like Gilbert, had married a young woman from Milwaukee in the 1880s, and the Gilberts knew the Seaburys very well. Seabury had recently been elected head of the Board of State Capitol Commissioners to create a new state house for Minnesota, and the legislature had appropriated two million dollars for the job. Cass told Seabury that he wanted to have a neighborly chat about the new state house.[29]

It may have been about this time that he paused at home one night to copy Ben Franklin's Almanac adage into his own diary: "The sleeping fox catches no poultry."

8

The Capitol

When the Minnesota legislature appointed its commission to build a new state capitol in 1891, neither legislators nor commissioners knew that the result would mark a decisive advance in the evolving history of this hallowed American building form.

Cass Gilbert bent every effort to achieve exactly that outcome. Here at last was his chance for enduring fame. His ambition now merged seamlessly with his newfound admiration for the neoclassical tradition, which had been confirmed by his look at Chicago's White City the year before. He intended to revitalize that tradition.

By the 1890s a full century had passed since neoclassical images first entered the American architectural imagination. They had arrived in the 1780s among the freshly unified states of post-revolutionary America. The neoclassical look created a mood that linked the ancient Roman republic to the new nation's republican rebellion from British monarchy. Among government buildings an early expression of the republican mood was Maryland's state house in Annapolis, crowned in 1785 by a stunning octagonal wooden dome crafted by Joseph Clark. Next, in Richmond, Virginia, Thomas Jefferson's state capitol, an adaptation of the ancient Roman temple form modeled after the Maison Carrée at Nîmes in the south of France, went up between 1785 and 1798. Meanwhile, Bostonians watched Charles Bulfinch's spherical dome rise from the broad portico of his new state house on Beacon Hill, built from 1795 to 1798 for the Commonwealth of Massachusetts.

Based on these models, the neoclassical domed temple became an ever more satisfying symbol of the young republic's proud aspirations. Examples of the form sprang up among state capitols across the pre–Civil War decades of the nineteenth century. The most influential of them were Gideon Shryock's Greek temple in Frankfort, Kentucky (1830); Maine's capitol in Augusta (1832), designed by the aging Bulfinch; the North Carolina capitol in Raleigh (1840), crafted by New York City partners Ithiel Town and Alexander Jackson Davis; and Vermont's golden-domed state house (1857, Thomas W. Silloway), set handsomely against its backdrop of dark green hills in the village of Montpelier.

The national capitol in Washington, begun in the mid-1790s, asserted the republican ideal from the outset. "We wish to exhibit a grandeur of conception, a republican simplicity, and that true elegance of proportion which corresponds to a tempered freedom excluding frivolity, the food of little minds," a spokesman for the new federal city declared.

The building on Capitol Hill expanded incrementally—north wing, south wing, central portico, and dome—under a succession of distinguished architects until its completion in 1825 in approximate accord with William Thornton's original design. But its soaring cast-iron central dome by Thomas U. Walter, replacing Thornton's more modest version, was not finished until the last year of the Civil War, seventy-one years after the building's cornerstone had been laid by President George Washington.[1]

In April 1865, the body of Abraham Lincoln lay in state beneath the new iron dome. Then his coffin began its solemn way west from Washington, pausing in the black-draped capitol buildings of New York, Pennsylvania, Ohio, and Indiana before reaching Lincoln's home in Springfield, Illinois. The symbolism of this journey was compelling for a grieving nation, as its murdered war leader passed among the temples of the republic he had saved. The journey momentarily turned an honored architectural tradition into something almost sacred.

In the architecture of post–Civil War America, however, nothing was durably sacred. As the Gothic revival moved into its gilded phase, supplanting or distorting classical appearances in public places, each element of the capitol building form was vertically distended to meet the mood of high Victorian striving. Meanwhile, new money, new governmental functions, new western states, and new industrial building materials combined to launch a heavy march of big new state capitols across the postwar era. The buildings were made of cast iron, pressed brick, ceramic tile, polished stone, molded sheet metals; they were grandiose, full of swagger, flaunting their deviance from classical proportions.

New York led this ostentatious parade with a building project that pounded along for some thirty years. The new capitol in Albany, originally under the charge of Canadian architect Thomas Fuller until patronage scandals prompted his dismissal in 1876, turned out to be a costly eclectic pile redeemed only by the talent of succeeding architects—H. H. Richardson and Leopold Eidlitz. They joined the project in the late 1870s to modify its exterior and rescue its interior spaces from mediocrity. In neighboring Connecticut, eight years of capitol construction produced the largest Gothic public building in America, designed by Richard Upjohn and completed in 1879. Further west a self-trained carpenter-turned-architect named Elijah Myers designed a trio of aggressive capitols for Michigan (1873–78), Texas (1881–88), and Colorado (1886–1908). A fellow practitioner cheerfully drew on Myers's Texas design for the Wyoming capitol (1886–90). In all these buildings, as well as in new capitols for Georgia, Illinois, Iowa, and Kansas, neoclassical elements were consistently warped in the vertical proportions of their domes, porticoes, and fenestration. Patriotic Texans could claim that the tall dome of their capitol, covered with zinc skin and supported by a lean iron frame rising from a limestone drum, actually reached seven feet higher than the dome of the national capitol in Washington. Myers and his fellow monument-makers of the Gilded Age were wonderfully skilled at generating splendor on the cheap.[2]

Cass Gilbert's determination to win the Minnesota capitol commission was sustained by a desire to transcend these gilded distortions and revive the salient neoclassical standards of the early republic: grandeur of conception and elegance of proportion, virtues now widely identified with the Parisian Beaux-Arts tradition. At the same time, he hoped to bring Minnesota abreast of relevant new benchmarks in the field, including the work done in Chicago's White City and that of his old firm, McKim, Mead and White. He admired in particular McKim's new Renaissance home for the Boston Public Library (1888–95) facing Richardson's Trinity Church across Copley Square, and he was alert to the firm's plans, published in 1892, for a new state capitol in Providence, Rhode Island. He had recently compiled a lantern slide lecture on classical architecture and identified the fifteenth-century Italian Renaissance as the "impulse of modern civilization." He hoped that the collective energies of his own time, "the natural result of the expanding intellect of the race"(like most contemporaries, he did not bother to define what he meant by "race"), were bringing on a comprehensive cultural rebirth. This in turn, he thought, was quickening the vitality of American architecture, however transitional and eclectic its recent past.[3]

Cass yearned to land the Minnesota job. He insisted also that the job be done right—that it be professionally correct. His instinct for the right way had been honed by fifteen years of bruising efforts to service the needs of powerful clients in the architectural arena. All too often in his experience, in the contest pitting architect against client, the architect—whether chosen by competition or invitation—suffered from the client's indifference to his training, talent, and standing. Cass fought hard against this demeaning political reality. His insistence on the professional status of his calling made him an aggressive member of the American Institute of Architects, whose Minnesota chapter he now chaired. The AIA had been founded in New York City back in 1857. After the Civil War, as its chapters and its influence spread westward, its leaders tried to promote respect for the architect's credentials, design fees, and contractual rights, including control over the execution of successful designs. Gilbert's insistent attention to these issues, together with his architectural prowess, had earned him a seat on the AIA's national board of directors in 1891.[4]

Gilbert wore the hat of the AIA when he went to see Commissioner Channing Seabury about the new Minnesota capitol in March 1894. Despite his long friendship with Seabury, he took a hard line on the project from the outset. In their initial chat, and in subsequent formal meetings with Seabury's capitol commission, he made clear not only his keen interest in landing the job but also the objections he shared with his AIA colleagues over the terms of the job. They thought the two million dollar budget ceiling imposed by the legislature on the project was woefully inadequate. They demanded their own close involvement in the design competition for selecting the architect. They wanted the architect's fee raised from 2.5 percent of construction costs to the AIA's standard fee of 5 percent. Most importantly they wanted the winning architect to control the construction process.[5]

Seabury's commission, exasperated by its inability to meet these demands without legislative consent, tried to hold an open design competition in the teeth of AIA protests. Gilbert and most of his colleagues refused to participate in this competition, as did most prominent out-of-state architects. Some fifty-six entries did arrive, predictably including one by Michigan's Elijah Myers, but none of any great merit. In January 1895 Seabury's commission announced that legislative restrictions had so badly marred the competitive process that a desirable choice was impossible. The architectural consultant chosen to judge the entries, Edmund Wheelwright of Boston (who like Gilbert had trained at MIT in the late 1870s and was familiar with and sympathetic to Gilbert's work) recommended that the commission scrap the first competition and move on to a second competition. Gilbert, having badgered Seabury and his commission tirelessly about the unsatisfactory terms of the first competition, was elated by Wheelwright's judgment, which was confirmed when the legislature then accepted the AIA's original demands governing a second competition. This new competition, which attracted forty-one entries including Gilbert's, got underway in the fall of 1895. Wheelwright's choice of five designs among those submitted included Gilbert's entry. After these finalists were thoroughly debated by Seabury's commission, Seabury accepted and enforced Wheelwright's recommendation that Gilbert be given the prize: "Cass Gilbert has won in this competition because of his superior talent, his strong personal character and standing in the community, his integrity and ability. . . . We have adopted the design which [Wheelwright] pointed out to us as being the best one submitted." (The entry submitted by Gilbert's erstwhile friend Clarence Johnston won fourth place in the second competition.)[6]

Gilbert now set to work honing the details of his entry. In place of a conventional classical pediment at the base of the capitol dome he positioned Daniel Chester French's Quadriga—four gilded horses and a charioteer symbolizing the Progress of the State. This was a revision of French's original Quadriga for the World's Columbian Exposition in Chicago. Gilbert's choice for the capitol dome itself turned out to be a virtual replica of the dome for St. Peters in Rome. The choice of stone for the dome lay between gray Minnesota granite (the overriding

St. Peter's of Rome, Vatican City, 1546–64.
(Photo by author)

parochial preference of local journalists and legislators, but "gloomy and forbidding" in Gilbert's view) or the sparkling white Georgia marble used by McKim, Mead and White in the Rhode Island capitol and strongly favored by Gilbert for Minnesota. "Its beautiful color, its brilliant crystalline structure, its facility in working, its strength under pressure, its durability in exposure to the atmosphere, and the immense quantities available, together with the moderate cost, make it in my opinion the most desirable material," he wrote. His preference prevailed. In response to local protest over the use of building materials from out of state, he argued forcefully: "Minnesota sells her wheat, lumber, iron, and other products all over the Union, and she is too great a State to surround herself with a Chinese wall which would exclude materials produced from without her borders. The best, no matter where produced, is none too good for Minnesota."[7]

Soon after winning this point, he set out to look over buildings he felt were relevant to his choice of white marble—the Rhode Island

Cass Gilbert with staff during construction of the capitol building, 1900.
(MHS Collections)

capitol (whose stone came from marble quarries at Tate, Georgia, near Atlanta, the ultimate source of the stone for the Minnesota dome as well) and the U.S. capitol and Library of Congress in Washington. To further inform his choices he began collecting books on the classical architecture of Greece, Rome, and France.

In December 1897 Gilbert launched a five-month trip to Belgium, Germany, Austria, and Italy with his wife, Julia, to examine continental structures he believed might anchor the details of the Minnesota capitol. In Berlin he found the latest modern German architecture, as exemplified by the new Reichstag, robust and strong and filled with useful lessons. His Italian stop included a climb into the dome of the cathedral in Florence to make notes about its construction. "This trip is a very valuable one for the Capitol work," he wrote, "as I am constantly finding practical points."[8]

Meanwhile, back in St. Paul in July 1898 the cornerstone of the capitol was set, and Gilbert's treatment for its interior mural program—crucial to the symbolic integrity of the structure—got underway. Six major muralists won his employment: John LaFarge, whose lunettes decorate the Supreme Court chamber, was dean of the group, which included also Kenyon Cox, Edward Simmons, H. O. Walker, and Edwin Blashfield. Blashfield's "Minnesota the Granary of the World" in the Senate chamber features a striking detail of patrons Cass Gilbert and Channing Seabury, a tribute to the force of their grand collaboration. The Governor's Reception Room in the west wing of the first floor, given over to mellow paintings from Minnesota history, is distinguished by Howard Pyle's "Battle of Nashville," which Gilbert told fellow architect Ralph Adams Cram was "absolutely one of the most remarkable pictures of modern times."[9]

The impact of the finished structure in St. Paul was stunning. One observer admired the "severe simplicity of Gilbert's design, whose strength lies in the symmetry of its proportions and the subordination of all ideas of ornamental detail to the general effect of the mass."[10]

In sum, it marked a decisive restoration of the pure neoclassical dimensions from which earlier state houses of the Gilded Age had

Minnesota State Capitol interior, view into dome.
(Photo by C. W. Jerome, MHS Collections)

strayed in their vertical distortions. Together with its marble cousin in Providence by McKim, Mead and White, it reestablished the virtues of republican order and harmony. In later years, Gilbert pursued these virtues in contests for capitols in Montana, Wisconsin, and Arkansas, climaxing in his West Virginia state house of the 1920s, the ultimate sunset model of the neoclassical domed temple that had emerged a century before in republican America. Thus his Minnesota capitol at last reached the apotheosis he had dreamed of a decade earlier, and his Twin Cities architectural career was complete.

Minnesota State Capitol interior, view down main stair toward rotunda.
(Photo by C. P. Gibson, MHS Collections)

Minnesota State Capitol interior, cantilevered stairway.
(Photo by Stan Waldhauser, MHS Collections)

F. W. Woolworth Company Building, New York, Cass Gilbert, 1910–13.
(View from the northeast, negative number 46309, © Collection of The New-York Historical Society)

EPILOGUE

In the years surrounding the turn of the century, the challenge of the skyscraper dominated Cass Gilbert's imagination. In February 1899 he sent his daughter Elizabeth a cartoon sketch that confessed his unguarded fascination with the height of tall buildings. He wrote playfully from Washington, "I think I shall build an office building down here somewhere. The buildings in New York are not high enough to suit me. The highest is only 33 stories. Now mine will look something like this. You see it is a good deal higher than the moon. It is so high that people going along the street don't look bigger than grass by comparison. You see it even goes up so high that I couldn't draw a line around it."

As things worked out, rather than introducing the skyscraper to Washington Gilbert elaborated on the form in the main home of its origin, New York City, designing Broadway Chambers and the West Street Building along the long and busy path to the Woolworth tower of 1913. "I am very busy here," he wrote from Manhattan to daughter Julia on March 28, 1899, "trying to pretend that I am the only one that knows how to plan buildings; but I know I am not & they know I know I am not but they are too polite to say so. So I go on pretending & in the meanwhile do the best I can to unload the cargo our ship has brought us. This is our ship & that blob at the back is me ahold of the tiller atrying to steer her into port. She's loaded with 'skyscrapers' & big buildings & is mighty hard to steer."

go down to the sea shore and bathe in the big waves, and dig clams and get sea shells & moss & all sorts of sea things.

So be happy my dear I think you will go east with me this spring or summer.

I think I shall build an office building down here somewhere. The buildings in New York are not high enough to suit me. The highest is only 33 stories. Now mine will look something like this; You see it is a good deal higher than the moon.

It is so high that the people going along the street don't look bigger than grass by comparison. You see it even goes up so high that I couldn't draw a line around it.

Give my love to each of the children and to Mother & kiss them all for me. Lovingly Your Father.

P.S. Tell mother I am in Washington & will return to New York tomorrow night, that I am well, and all right.

(above) *From letter to Elizabeth Gilbert, February 20, 1899.*
(Gilbert Papers, Library of Congress)

(facing page) *From letter to Julia Gilbert, March 28, 1899.*
(Gilbert Papers, Library of Congress)

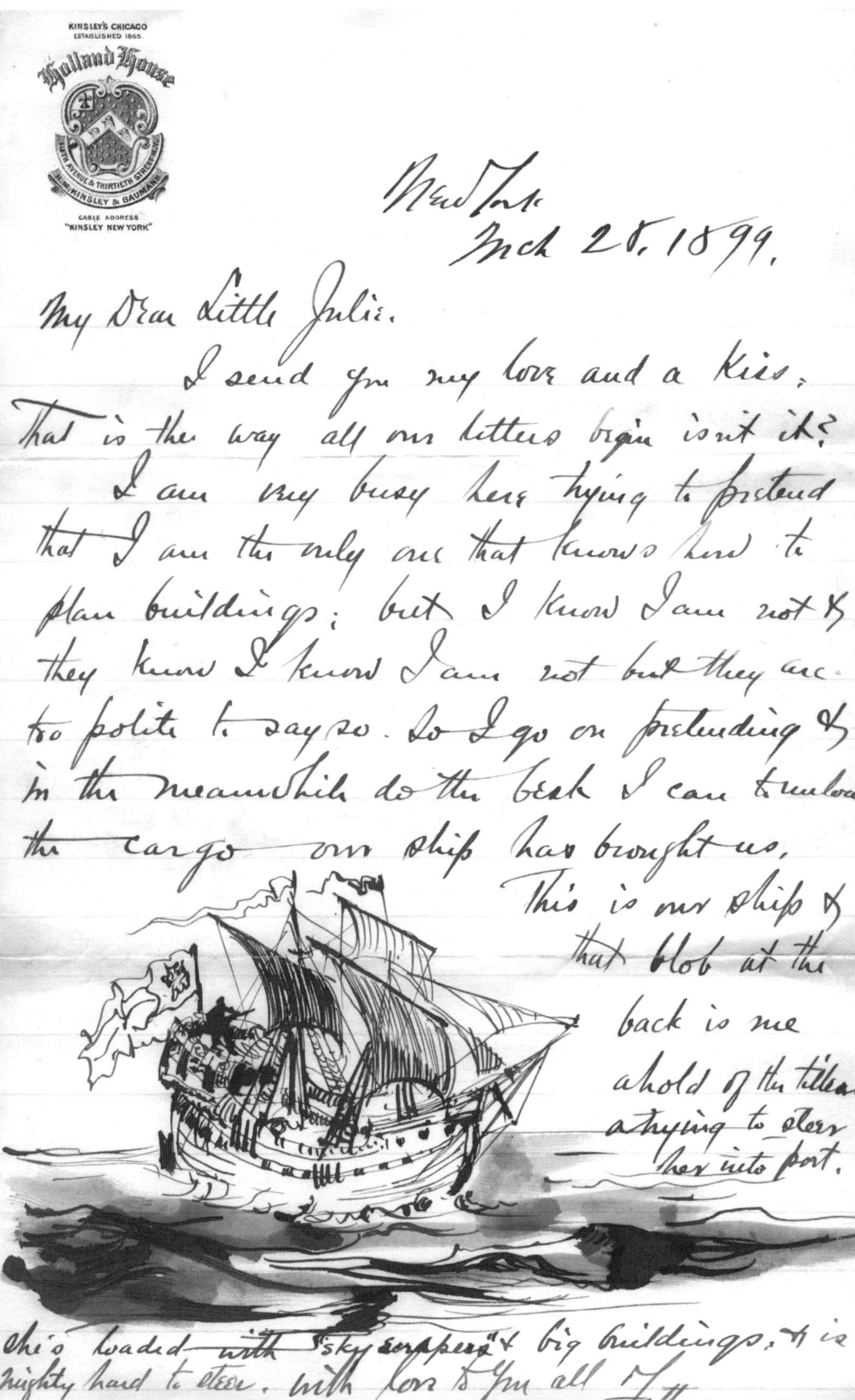

KINSLEY'S CHICAGO
ESTABLISHED 1865.
Holland House
FIFTH AVENUE & THIRTIETH STREET N.Y.
KINSLEY & BAUMANN
CABLE ADDRESS
"KINSLEY NEW YORK"

New York
Mch 28. 1899.

My Dear Little Julie:

I send you my love and a kiss: That is the way all our letters begin isn't it?

I am very busy here trying to pretend that I am the only one that knows how to plan buildings; but I know I am not & they know I know I am not but they are too polite to say so. So I go on pretending & in the meanwhile do the best I can to unload the cargo our ship has brought us.

This is our ship & that blob at the back is me ahold of the tiller a trying to steer her into port.

She's loaded with "sky scrapers" & big buildings & it is mighty hard to steer. With love to you all

Father.

On September 24, 1899, Cass recorded his victory over Carrere and Hastings and fourteen other Manhattan firms in the competition to design the United States Custom House, which would overlook Bowling Green in New York harbor. Again the metaphor was nautical: A letter home to his wife, Julia, showed their ship approaching the Statue of Liberty with the triumphant inscription, "Our ship's come in. She's in the harbor now."

United States Custom House, New York, Cass Gilbert, 1899–1907.
(Exterior from Bowling Green, ca. 1908, G. P. Hall & Sons Collection, negative number 59216, © Collection of The New-York Historical Society)

In 1900, his business in St. Paul having dwindled severely and prospects in Manhattan continuing to look up, Cass made a decisive residential departure to New York's Upper East Side. He had been reluctant to move his four children from the freedom and comfort of St. Paul to the big city, but self-mocking phrases about his "Siberian exile" from the "effete East" confirmed the allure of New York. "In the new life in New York," he wrote to his wife, "we hope for a larger opportunity for ourselves and our children—for bigger buildings and more of them, and consequently for a larger income, that will enable us to put something aside for the future. We feel that in St. Paul when the Capitol is finished it will be unlikely that other important works will go forward there, and that if we remain I may find my professional work come to a stop with its completion. An opportunity appears to await us here that promises great success and we would be wrong to neglect it. New York is the center for my kind of work, it has a fine climate, it affords opportunities for enjoying music, art, society and all that makes modern life in cities desirable."[1]

Ambivalence in Gilbert's attitudes toward east and west would never disappear, however. "I highly regard your advice as to remaining a western man," he told his brother, Charles, in 1902. "I am so in spirit . . . though to all intents and purposes I now hail from New York." Not until 1910, with work on the details of the Minnesota capitol decisively complete, did he close his St. Paul office in favor of New York. A year later, while arranging for his son to summer in the Rockies, he confessed that "I was brought up in the west myself and I want him to see something of the same sort of life before he grows to full manhood." For all the appeal of Manhattan, and his new fascination with the challenge of its skyscrapers, the tug of the west and the psychological legacy of St. Paul remained durably intact.[2]

His Minnesota years also left indelible marks on the architecture he pursued into the twentieth century—not only along the way to Woolworth but in big neoclassical library commissions like St. Louis and Detroit and campuses like the picturesque collection at Oberlin, culminating in his last great commission, the United States Supreme Court building in Washington, D.C. His steady preoccupation with

Detroit Public Library, Cass Gilbert, 1913–21.
(Burton Historical Collection, Detroit Public Library)

West façade, United States Supreme Court Building, Washington, D.C., Cass Gilbert, 1928–35.
(Photograph by Franz Jantzen, Collection of the Supreme Court of the United States)

the beautiful, whether defined in neoclassical appearances or the picturesque, remained intact from his final decade in St. Paul, as did the resilient drive with which he satisfied his clients, including his knack for applying ideas from his travels to meet their demands. Despite the reversals that clouded his reputation with the arrival of the modern during his last years, he clung to a faith in the lasting integrity of his creations. Into the back of his diary of 1932 he carefully copied the inscription he found on the frieze of the rotunda in London's National Gallery: "The works of those who have stood the test of the ages have a claim to that respect and veneration to which no modern can pretend." Cass Gilbert wanted very much to believe that about himself. The long totality of his career, from St. Paul forward, clearly justified this faith.[3]

Cass Gilbert, 1907.
(Photo by Pach of New York, MHS Collections)

NOTES

NOTE TO INTRODUCTION

1. Benjamin Franklin, *Poor Richard's Almanac* (New York: David McKay, Reprinted 1973), 9, prefixed to Almanac of 1757. Franklin's adage is quoted in Cass Gilbert Diary, New-York Historical Society (hereafter, NYHS), dated 1891 and extended several years thereafter.

NOTES TO CHAPTER 1

1. Frank B. Woodford, *Lewis Cass: The Last Jeffersonian* (New Brunswick: Rutgers University Press, 1950), passim.
2. Cass Gilbert to Francis Swales, Sept. 24, 1909, box 9, Gilbert Papers, Library of Congress (hereafter, LC).
3. Charles C. Gilbert to Peyton Gilbert, Feb. 24, 1846 and Sept. 9, 1850; Samuel Gilbert to Peyton Gilbert, Nov. 28, 1854; Cass Gilbert to Swales, Sept. 24, 1909, Gilbert Papers, LC; Cass Gilbert to Henry Churchill King, Dec. 19, 1903, King Papers, Oberlin College Archives (hereafter, OCA).
4. Cass Gilbert to Frank Bacon, July 25, 1927, box 12, Gilbert Papers, LC; Cass Gilbert to L. V. H. Black, May 24, 1905, Gilbert Letterbook, OCA.
5. Sharon Irish, *Cass Gilbert's Career in New York, 1899–1905* (Ann Arbor: University Microfilms, 1985), 35–37; Elizabeth W. Gilbert to Cass Gilbert, June 23 (n.d.), box 18, Cass Gilbert Papers, Minnesota Historical Society (hereafter, MHS).
6. The best brief introduction to the early history of the Twin Cities remains the New Deal's Federal Writers Project volume, *Minnesota: A State Guide* (New York: Viking Press, 1938), 153–234. A more thorough study is Theodore Blegen, *Minnesota: A History of the State* (St. Paul: University of Minnesota Press, 1975). Mark Twain is quoted from his *Life on the Mississippi* (New York: Harper Stormfield Edition, 1929), 491. For Summit Avenue, see Ernest R. Sandeen, *St. Paul's Historic Summit Avenue* (St. Paul: Macalester College, 1978), 1–7.
7. Elizabeth Gilbert to Cass Gilbert, June 23 (n.d.), box 18; Cass Gilbert to E. S. Hall, Oct. 20, 1908, box 20, Gilbert Papers, MHS.
8. Elizabeth Gilbert to Cass Gilbert, Nov. 24, 1878, Gilbert Papers, LC; *St. Paul Pioneer Press*, May 24, 1934.
9. Irish, *Cass Gilbert's Career*, 36; Cass Gilbert to John Rich, July 10, 1919, Letterbook, OCA.

10. Paul Clifford Larson, *Minnesota Architect: The Life and Work of Clarence H. Johnston* (Afton, Minn.: Afton Historical Society Press, 1996), 5–7; Cass Gilbert Diary, Mar. 19, 1922, Gilbert Papers, LC; Cass Gilbert to Clarence Johnston, Jan. 16, 1879, Johnston Papers, MHS. For the early years of *American Architect and Building News*, see Mary Woods, "History in the Early American Architectural Journals," *The Architectural Historian in America*, Elizabeth B. MacDougall, ed. (Hanover: University Press of New England, 1990), 81–85.

11. Cass Gilbert to Clarence Johnston, July 11, 1878, Clarence H. Johnston Papers, MHS.

NOTES TO CHAPTER 2

1. Larson, *Minnesota Architect*, 7; Walter Muir Whitehill, *Boston: A Topographical History* (Cambridge: Harvard University Press, 1959), 169, 189; Samuel C. Prescott, *When MIT was "Boston Tech," 1861–1916* (Cambridge: Technology Press, 1954), 50–67. For a good brief discussion of Trinity Church, see Susan and Michael Southworth, *A.I.A. Guide to Boston* (Chester, Conn.: Globe Pequot Press, 1984), 217–22.

2. William R. Ware, *Outline of Architectural Instruction* (Boston: Press of John Wilson, 1866), 6. Brief summaries of Ware's career appear in the *National Cyclopaedia of American Biography* (New York: James T. White & Co., 1924), vol. 8, 440–41; *Dictionary of American Biography* (New York: Scribner's, 1936), vol. 19, 452–53; and *Macmillan Encyclopedia of Architects* (New York: Free Press, 1982), vol. 4, 373–74. See also David G. DeLong, "William R. Ware and the Pursuit of Suitability: 1881–1903," *The Making of an Architect, 1881–1981: Columbia University in the City of New York,* Richard Oliver, ed. (New York: Rizzoli, 1981), 13–21.

3. This point is elaborated at length in Donald Drew Egbert, *The Beaux-Arts Tradition in French Architecture* (Princeton: Princeton University Press, 1980), 58–86. In 1927 the French modernist Le Corbusier wrote of the Ecole, "As time has gone by, dogmas have been established, and recipes and tricks. A method of teaching useful enough at the beginning has become a dangerous practice." Le Corbusier, *Towards a New Architecture* (London: The Architectural Press, 1927), 165, 166.

4. Richard Chafee, "The Teaching of Architecture at the Ecole Des Beaux-Arts," *The Architecture of the Ecole des Beaux-Arts,* Arthur Drexler, ed. (Cambridge: MIT Press, 1977), 75–109; Franz Schulze, "Architecture of the Beaux-Arts," *Art News*, 75 (Jan. 1976), 86–87; James Noffsinger, *The Influence of the Ecole des Beaux-Arts on the Architects of the United States* (Washington: Catholic University of America Press, 1955), 11–42; A. D. F. Hamlin, "The Influence of the Ecole des Beaux-Arts on Our Architectural Education," *Architectural Record,* 23:4 (Apr. 1908), 241–47.

5. Douglass Shand-Tucci, *Built in Boston, City and Suburb* (Amherst: University of Massachusetts Press, 1988), Ch. 2. For Ware's introduction to classicism by Hunt, see his Preface to *The American Vignola* (Scranton: International Textbook Co., 1902), iii. For his remark about pine Parthenons, see Ware, *Outline*, 22–23.

6. Mary N. Woods, "History in the Early American Architectural Journals," *The Architectural Historian in America*, Elizabeth MacDougall, ed., 82–84.

7. Cass Gilbert to Clarence Johnston, Oct. 25, 1879, Johnston Papers, MHS.

8. Cass Gilbert to Clarence Johnston, Jan. 5, 1879, Johnston Papers, MHS.

9. Cass Gilbert to Clarence Johnston, Jan. 16, 1879, May 29, 1879, and June 22, 1879, Johnston Papers, MHS.

10. Cass Gilbert to Clarence Johnston, Jan. 16, 1879 and June 22, 1879, Johnston Papers.

11. Cass Gilbert, handwritten memorandum, Apr. 26, 1886, Gilbert Papers, LC; Louis Sullivan, *The Autobiography of an Idea* (New York: Press of the AIA, 1924), 185, 188; Cass Gilbert to Clarence Johnston, Jan. 16, 1879, Johnston Papers, MHS.

12. Albert Rosengarten, *A Handbook of Architectural Styles,* translated from the German by W. Collett-Sandars, with Preface by T. Roger Smith (New York: D. Appleton & Co., 1876), v, vi.

13. Sullivan, *Autobiography*, 187; "A Master and His Pupils," *American Architect and Building News (AABN),* 83:1462 (Jan. 2, 1904), 19–20.

14. Cass Gilbert to Clarence Johnston, July 21, 1879, Johnston Papers, MHS.

15. Sullivan, *Autobiography*, 185, 189; Cass Gilbert to Clarence Johnston, Jan. 5, 1879, May 29, 1879, and June 22, 1879, Johnston Papers, MHS.

16. Cass Gilbert to Clarence Johnston, Jan. 16, 1879, Feb. 5, 1879, and June 22, 1879, Johnston Papers, MHS.

17. Cass Gilbert to DeLisle Stewart, Jan. 26, 1914, Gilbert Papers, LC.

18. Cass Gilbert to Clarence Johnston, Feb. 5, 1879 and May 29, 1879, Johnston Papers, MHS; Cass Gilbert to S. E. Mezes, Jan. 20, 1910, Gilbert Letterbooks, OCA. Like Gilbert, Arnold Brunner would spend the bulk of his career in New York City producing monumental public buildings of classical design.

19. Cass Gilbert to Clarence Johnston, June 22, July 5, and Aug. 26, 1879, Johnston Papers, MHS. Gilbert was of course not alone in his attraction to the prominent London architects of the 1870s and their stylistic mood. Another Ware student recalled that "the arguments that vexed us then, the great question of the English Gothic School or the French Classics, [were] so alive then that one longed to have been born in either pale and so to have escaped the burden of a choice. . . . Then we found that in the country of Street and Scott and Burges and Shaw, the country that seemed most like home to us, practically nobody was doing any Classic work. . . ." "A Master and His Pupils," *AABN*, 19.

20. Cass Gilbert to Clarence Johnston, Aug. 26, 1879, Oct. 25, 1879, and Nov. 17, 1879.

NOTES TO CHAPTER 3

1. Henry James, *A Little Tour in France* (Boston: Houghton Mifflin, 1900), 1. For the origins and functions of the tour, see William E. Mead, *The Grand Tour in the Eighteenth Century* (Boston: Houghton Mifflin, 1914), Ch. 1 and passim. For the meaning of the tour among nineteenth-century American writers, see William W. Stowe, *Going Abroad: European Travel in Nineteenth-Century American Culture* (Princeton: Princeton University Press, 1994), Chs. 1–3.

2. Cass Gilbert to Clarence Johnston, Oct. 25, 1879, MHS. The letters of introduction Cass carried with him to Europe in 1880 are in box 2, Gilbert Papers, LC.

3. Cass Gilbert to Clarence Johnston, Aug. 26, 1879 and Dec. 16, 1879, Johnston Papers, MHS. For the Albany Capitol project, see essays by Geoffrey Blodgett, Albert Fein, and William Seale in *Proceedings of the New York State Capitol Symposium* (Albany: Temporary State Commission on the Restoration of the Capitol, 1983).

4. Cass Gilbert to Elizabeth Gilbert, Jan. 18, 1880, Gilbert Papers, LC.

5. Cass Gilbert to Elizabeth Gilbert, Jan. 28, 1880 and Feb. 1, 1880, Gilbert Papers, LC; Cass Gilbert to Clarence Johnston, Jan. 30, 1880 and Mar. 21, 1880, Johnston Papers, MHS; Julia Finch Gilbert, ed., *Cass Gilbert: Reminiscences and Addresses* (New York: privately printed, 1935), 39.

6. Cass Gilbert to Clarence Johnston, Jan. 30, 1880, Johnston Papers, MHS.

7. Cass Gilbert to Elizabeth Gilbert, Jan. 24, 1880, Gilbert Papers, LC. The year before, when some young architects in the Boston office of Peabody and Stearns asked Gilbert how he liked the new "colonial" style, he had replied that he disliked many aspects of it and further noted that "they evidently are on the 'ragged edge' themselves about it." Cass Gilbert to Clarence Johnston, Jan. 30, 1880, Johnston Papers, MHS.

8. Cass Gilbert to Elizabeth Gilbert, Feb. 6, 1880, Gilbert Papers, LC. For one veteran's impression of the city in 1880, see Harriet Keeler, *The Life of Adelia A. Field Johnston* (Cleveland: Korner & Wood, 1912), 120. On the mood of the Ecole, see *Inland Architect and News Record,* 17:5 (June 1891).

9. Cass Gilbert to Elizabeth Gilbert, Feb. 1, 6, 1880, Gilbert Papers, LC; Cass Gilbert to Clarence Johnston, Mar. 21, 1880, Johnston Papers, MHS. *A Handbook for Visitors to Paris* (London: John Murray, 1874) guides its reader through the Paris Gilbert visited.

10. Cass Gilbert to Elizabeth Gilbert, Feb. 14, 19, and Mar. 4–16, 1880, Gilbert Papers, LC.

11. Cass Gilbert to Elizabeth Gilbert, Mar. 4, 1880, Gilbert Papers, LC.

12. Cass Gilbert to Clarence Johnston, Mar. 21, 1880, Johnston Papers, MHS.

13. Cass Gilbert to Elizabeth Gilbert, Mar. 22 and Apr. 3, 1880, Gilbert Papers, LC.

14. Cass Gilbert to Elizabeth Gilbert, Mar. 22, 28, Apr. 3, 10, and 24, 1880, Gilbert Papers, LC.

15. Cass Gilbert to Elizabeth Gilbert, Apr. 10, 24, 1880, Gilbert Papers, LC.

16. Cass Gilbert to Elizabeth Gilbert, May 9, 1880, Gilbert Papers, LC.

17. Cass Gilbert to Elizabeth Gilbert, July 18, 1880, Gilbert Papers, LC; Cass Gilbert to Clarence Johnston, July 18, 1880, Johnston Papers, MHS; Peter Mathias, *The First Industrial Nation: An Economic History of Britain, 1700–1914* (London: Methuen & Co., 1969), 395, 398; R. C. K. Ensor, *England, 1870–1914* (Oxford: Clarenden Press, 1936), 111–12; Frances Swales, "Master Draftsmen: Cass Gilbert," *Pencil Points*, 7:10 (Oct. 1926), 583.

NOTES TO CHAPTER 4

1. Cass Gilbert, handwritten memorandum, Sept. 7, 1927, Gilbert Papers, LC.

2. Leland Roth, *McKim, Mead & White, Architects* (New York: Harper & Row, 1983), 17–66; Paul R. Baker, *Stanny: The Gilded Life of Stanford White* (New York: Free Press, 1989), 59–89; Richard Guy Wilson, *McKim, Mead & White, Architects* (New York: Rizzoli, 1983), 9–16; Charles Baldwin, *Stanford White* (New York: Dodd, Mead, 1931), Chs. 5 and 16; Harry Carlson to Cass Gilbert, Nov. 17, 1891, Gilbert Papers, MHS.

3. Harriet Moore, *John Wellborn Root, Architect* (Boston: Houghton Mifflin, 1896), 65.

4. H. Van Buren Magonigle, "A Half Century of Architecture," 2, *Pencil Points*, 15:1 (Jan. 1934), 11; Wheeler Dow, *American Renaissance: A Review of Domestic Architecture* (New York: William T. Comstock, 1904), 111.

5. Montgomery Schuyler, *American Architecture & Other Writing*, William Jordy and Ralph Coe, eds. (New York: Atheneum, 1964), 63–64, 81; Mariana van Rensselaer, "Recent Architecture in America," *Century*, 28:1 (May 1884), 53–61. See also Dow, *American Renaissance*, 27–29.

6. *AABN*, 9:277 (Apr. 16, 1881), 183; Charles Dudley Warner, *Their Pilgrimage* (New York: Harper, 1886), 87; J. S. Ingram, *The Centennial Exposition, Described and*

Illustrated (Philadelphia: Hubbard Bros., 1876), 567–69, 604–10, 636–37, 706–8, 716–18; Vincent Scully, *The Shingle Style* (New Haven: Yale University Press, 1955), Ch. 2; William B. Rhoads, *The Colonial Revival* (New York: Garland, 1977), 23, 51, 56–64. Rhoads tracks the pre-centennial origins of the post-war colonial revival to a paper read by Richard Upjohn to the 1869 annual meeting of the AIA and to the house that Richard Morris Hunt built for himself in Newport, Rhode Island, in 1870.

7. Charles Moore, *The Life and Times of Charles Follen McKim* (Boston: Houghton Mifflin, 1929), 41; Scully, *Shingle Style*; Scully, *The Architecture of the American Summer* (New York: Rizzoli, 1989); Rhoads, *Colonial Revival*, 65–67; Shand-Tucci, *Built in Boston*, 65–72.

8. Francis Swales, "Cass Gilbert," *Pencil Points*, 7:10 (Oct. 1926), 583; Leland Roth, *The Architecture of McKim, Mead & White, 1870–1920: A Building List* (New York: Garland, 1978), 67–69, 112.

9. William Mead to Cass Gilbert, Apr. 6, 1882, Francis Bacon to Cass Gilbert, Oct. 2, 1882, Cass Gilbert to Francis Bacon, July 25, 1927, Gilbert Papers, LC; Antoinette Downing and Vincent Scully, *The Architectural Heritage of Newport Rhode Island* (New York: Clarkson N. Potter, 1967), 161–64; Baker, *Stanny*, 66–68, 72; Wayne Andrews, *Architecture, Ambitions, and Americans* (New York: Free Press, 1978).

10. Cass Gilbert entry, Jan. 10, 1922, 1922 Diary, Gilbert Papers, LC; H. Van Buren Magonigle, "A Half Century of Architecture," 3, *Pencil Points* (Mar. 1934), 117; Cass Gilbert, handwritten memorandum, Sept. 7, 1927, Gilbert Papers, LC; Walter Tittle, "The Creator of the Woolworth Tower," *World's Work*, 54 (May 1927), 101; Burke Wilkinson, *The Life and Works of Augustus Saint Gaudens* (New York: Dover, 1992), 105–6, 112, 127, 131.

11. Cass Gilbert, handwritten memorandum, Sept. 7, 1927, Gilbert Papers, LC.

12. For a discussion of scenographic architecture, see William Hubbard, *Complicity and Convention: Steps Toward an Architecture of Convention* (Cambridge: MIT Press, 1980), 12–49.

13. Roth, *McKim, Mead & White*, 66; H. Van Buren Magonigle, "A Half Century of Architecture," 1, *Pencil Points* (Nov. 1933), 479.

14. Cass Gilbert to Julia Finch, Jan. 3, 1887, Cass Gilbert to Frank Bacon, July 27, 1927, Gilbert Papers, LC.

15. Larson, *Minnesota Architect*, 16–18; Cass Gilbert, "Architectural League of New York," typescript, Mar. 23, 1931, Gilbert Papers, LC.

16. Roth, *Architecture of McKim, Mead & White*, 26 and Plate 97; Roger Riordan, "The Architectural League of New York," *Century*, 25:4 (Feb. 1883); Richard Grant White, "Old New York and its Houses, *Century*, 26:6 (Oct. 1883).

17. William Mead to Cass Gilbert, Apr. 6, 1882, Gilbert Papers, LC; "Recent Building in Baltimore," *AABN*, 12:355 (Oct. 14, 1882), 182–83; Wilson, *McKim, Mead & White*, 16, 84–87.

18. Cass Gilbert to Clarence Johnston, Aug. 6, 1882, Johnston Papers, MHS.

19. Cass Gilbert to Clarence Johnston, Aug. 24, 1882, Johnston Papers, MHS; John Scarff, ed., *The Bicentennial Celebration of the Birth of Charles Carroll of Carrollton, 1737–1937* (Baltimore: Lord Baltimore Press, [1938]), 18, 132.

20. Cass Gilbert to Clarence Johnston, Aug. 24, 1882.

21. Baldwin, *White*, 357–68; Wilson, *McKim, Mead & White*, 16–17; Roth, *McKim, Mead & White*, 86–87; Joseph M. Wells to Cass Gilbert, Feb. 4, 1883 and July 30, 1884, Cass Gilbert to Julia Finch, Dec. 16, 1886, Gilbert Papers, LC.

22. Cass Gilbert to Elizabeth Gilbert, Mar. 28, 1880 and May 23, 1880, Elizabeth Gilbert to Cass Gilbert, Jan. 25, 1882, Gilbert Papers, LC; Cass Gilbert to Clarence Johnston, Aug. 24, 1882, Johnston Papers, MHS.

23. Joseph M. Wells to Cass Gilbert, Feb. 4, 1883, Gilbert Papers, LC.

24. Cass Gilbert to John Beverly Robinson, Sept. 25, 1891, Gilbert Papers, MHS.

25. Cass Gilbert to Francis H. Bacon, Mar. 31, 1911, Gilbert Papers, LC.

NOTES TO CHAPTER 5

1. Larson, *Minnesota Architect*, 23, 27.

2. Larry Millett, *Lost Twin Cities* (St. Paul: Minnesota Historical Society Press, 1992), 50, 107, 110. The competition for commissions in a growth environment kept Gilbert, Taylor, and Johnston constantly alert and anxious. When a local building inspector publicly criticized the inexperience of St. Paul's younger architects, they called the charge "unwarranted, false and libelous," and demanded a retraction. See *Inland Architect and Builder*, 4:5 (June 1885).

3. Millett, *Lost Twin Cities*, 49, 109, 128. Decisive suburban sprawl awaited replacement of the trolley by the automobile. Nineteenth-century mansions along Summit Avenue and adjacent streets occupied much smaller sites than do homes in twentieth-century automobile suburbs, and many of the earlier homes still lack space for driveways and garages.

4. A vivid discussion of the servant problem may be found in Mrs. John Sherwood, *Manners and Social Usages* (New York: Harper, 1887). See for example p. 374: "The harassed and troubled American woman who has to cope with the worst servants in the world—the ill-trained, incapable, and vicious peasantry to Europe, who come here to be 'as good as anybody,' and who see that it is easily possible to make a living in America whether they are respectful or not—that woman has a very arduous task to perform."

5. For window screens, see Alan Gowans, *The Comfortable House: North American Suburban Architecture, 1890–1930* (Cambridge: MIT Press, 1986), 28.

6. Cass Gilbert to H. Weatherby, Dec. 21, 1900, Cass Gilbert Letterbook, Gilbert Papers, NYHS. According to one contemporary observer, "the dwelling is the most pottering and worst-paid work an architect ever does." *Inland Architect and News Record*, 17:2 (Mar. 1891). For further exploration of the themes discussed in this paragraph, see Clifford Clark, Jr., "Domestic Architecture as an Index to Social History," *Journal of Interdisciplinary History*, 7:1 (Summer 1976), 33–56; David Handlin, *The American Home: Architecture and Society, 1815–1900* (Boston: Little, Brown, 1979), Ch. 1; and Colleen McDannell, *The Christian Home in Victorian America, 1840–1900* (Bloomington: Indiana University Press, 1986), Chs. 2 and 3.

7. Larson, *Minnesota Architect*, 5, 26, 27.

8. Roth, *McKim, Mead & White*, 85–94; William R. Mead to Cass Gilbert, June 12, 15, 22, 1883, Gilbert Papers, MHS; Henry Haupt to Marquis de Mans, June 19, 1884, Gilbert Papers, LC; Cass Gilbert to Mr. Kirby, Jan. 26, 1884, Gilbert Papers, NYHS.

9. Millett, *Lost Twin Cities*, 124.

10. Roth, *McKim, Mead & White*, 91–92; Cass Gilbert to Mr. Kirby, Jan. 26, 1884, Gilbert Papers, NYHS.

11. Patricia Murphy, "The Early Career of Cass Gilbert: 1878 to 1895" (master's thesis, University of Virginia, 1979), includes a detailed analysis of Gilbert's club memberships in St. Paul.

12. Larson, *Minnesota Architect*, 44; Ernest R. Sandeen, *St. Paul's Historic Summit*

Avenue (St. Paul: Macalester College, 1978), 76–77; Cass Gilbert to Julia Finch, Oct. 25, 1886, Gilbert Papers, LC; Cass Gilbert to "Dear Sir," Mar. 15, 1884, Cass Gilbert Letterbook, Gilbert Papers, NYHS.

13. Patricia Murphy, *Cass Gilbert: Ramsey Hill House Tour* (St. Paul: Ramsey Hill Association, 1981), 2; Cass Gilbert to Mr. Kirby, Jan. 26, 1884, Gilbert Papers, NYHS; Cass Gilbert to Julia Finch, Sept. 7, 1886, Gilbert Papers, LC. The hospitality of owner Marilyn Vogel, who invited me to look over the interior of 471 Ashland in June 1999, is gratefully remembered.

14. Murphy, *Gilbert*, 2, 5, 7; Cass Gilbert to Julia Finch, June 24, 1887, Gilbert Papers, LC.

15. Cass Gilbert to John LaFarge, Sept. 27, 1884, Cass Gilbert Letterbook, Gilbert Papers, NYHS. See John W. Root, "The City House in the West," *Scribner's Magazine*, 8:4 (Oct. 1890), 416–34. Root stressed the relative variety, autonomy, and simplicity of western urban residences, and illustrated his article with one of Gilbert's early wood-frame houses in St. Paul.

16. Current owners Hugh Huestler and Jean Tierney gave me a thorough tour of their house, gardens, and shingled stables in July 1998.

17. A. H. S. Perkins, *All About White Bear Lake* (White Bear, Minn.: 1890), 3–26; Michael Conforti, ed., *Art and Life on the Upper Mississippi, 1890–1915* (Newark: University of Delaware Press, 1994), 35, 56–57; Vincent Scully, *The Architecture of the American Summer*, 122; Jan Forsberg to author, Aug. 15 and Sept. 14, 1997. I am indebted to Ms. Forsberg for tracking down important details about the surviving Cass Gilbert houses on White Bear Lake. Ellen Fridinger, current owner of the Tarbox house on Manitou Island, graciously hosted several visits to her home in summer 1999.

18. Roth, *McKim, Mead & White*, 96–97; Arnold Lewis, *American Country Houses of the Gilded Age* (New York: Dover, 1982), plate 53; Murphy, *Cass Gilbert*, 3, 5, 6; Cass Gilbert to Julia Finch, Apr. 12, 1887, Gilbert Papers, LC.

19. Murphy, *Gilbert*, 6, 7; Sandeen, *Summit Avenue*, 56, 57, 82; Conforti, ed., *Art and Life*, 36–37, 57. The Lionberger house was illustrated in *Inland Architect and News Record*, 11:7 (June 1888).

20. Larson, *Minnesota Architect*, 35–37; Sandeen, *Summit Avenue*, 94, 99–107. See Jan Cigliano's essay on Euclid Avenue and Mary Alice Molloy's essay on Prairie Avenue in *The Grand Avenue, 1850–1920,* Jan Cigliano and Sarah Bradford Landau, eds. (San Francisco: Pomegranate Art Books, 1994), 93–151.

21. Cass Gilbert to E. C. Simmons, June 4, 1907, Cass Gilbert to W. A. Johnson, Feb. 19, 1910, Cass Gilbert Letterbooks, OCA; *St. Paul Pioneer Press Dispatch*, May 23, 1988; Montgomery Schuyler, "Glimpses of Western Architecture: St. Paul and Minneapolis," *Harper's Monthly*, 83:497 (Oct. 1891), 740–41; Cass Gilbert to Julia Finch, Oct. 13, 1886, Gilbert Papers, LC.

22. Murphy, *Cass Gilbert*, 7; David Gebhard and Tom Martinson, *A Guide to the Architecture of Minnesota* (Minneapolis: University of Minnesota Press, 1977), 106, 224; W. Walton to Cass Gilbert, May 28, 1898, Gilbert Papers, MHS. On this letter from the rector of Moorhead's Church of St. John the Divine, Gilbert sketched a preliminary plan and perspective drawing for the church.

23. Gebhart and Martinson, *Guide*, 128.

24. Gebhard and Martinson, *Guide*, 101; Murphy, *Cass Gilbert*, 5.

25. Mrs. Theodore Eaton to M. N. Gilbert, June 18, 1894, Cass Gilbert to E. P. Woodruff, Jan. 5, 1911, Gilbert Papers, MHS; Cass Gilbert to E. Mary Appleby, Dec. 15, 1930, Cass Gilbert Letterbook, Gilbert Papers, NYHS.

26. Cass Gilbert to Julia Finch, Mar. 27, 1887, Gilbert Papers, LC; Paula Petrik, *No Step Backward: Women and Family on the Rocky Mountain Mining Frontier, 1865–1900* (Helena: Montana Historical Society Press, 1987), Ch. 1.

27. Cass Gilbert to Julia Finch, Mar. 31, 1887, Gilbert Papers, LC.

28. William Dean Howells, *The Rise of Silas Lapham* (Boston: Ticknor & Co., 1885), 55–57; *New York Times*, Mar. 25, 1917.

29. Cass Gilbert to Julia Finch, Oct. 20 and Dec.16, 1886, Gilbert Papers, LC.

NOTES TO CHAPTER 6

1. Julia Finch to Cass Gilbert, Sept. 5, 1886, Elizabeth Gilbert to her sister, Nov. 28, 1886, Cass Gilbert to Julia Finch, Feb. 14, 1887 and May 19, 1889, Gilbert Papers, LC.

2. Julia Finch to Cass Gilbert, [Sept. 1886], Gilbert Papers, LC; Ellen Rothman, *Hands and Hearts: A History of Courtship in America* (New York: Basic Books, 1984), Introduction and Ch. 6; Karen Lystra, *Searching the Heart: Women, Men, and Romantic Love in Nineteenth-Century America* (New York: Oxford University Press, 1989), Chs. 2 and 6.

3. Julia Finch to Cass Gilbert, [Aug. 1886], Nov. 27, [1886], and Mar. 11, 1887, Elizabeth Gilbert to her sister, Nov. 28, 1886, Gilbert Papers, LC.

4. Julia Finch to Cass Gilbert, Oct. 11, [1886], Cass Gilbert to Julia Finch, Jan. 3, 1887, Gilbert Papers, LC.

5. Julia Finch to Cass Gilbert, Oct. 3, Nov. 1, and Dec. 25, [1886], Mar. 24 and Oct. 16, 1887, Gilbert Papers, LC.

6. Julia Finch to Cass Gilbert, Sept. 17 and Nov. 1, [1886], Cass Gilbert to Julia Finch, Oct. 19, 1886, Gilbert Papers, LC.

7. Cass Gilbert to Julia Finch, Dec. 1, 1886, Julia Finch to Cass Gilbert, Dec. 12, [1886], Gilbert Papers, LC.

8. Cass Gilbert to Julia Finch, Sept. 12, 1886, Gilbert Papers, LC.

9. Cass Gilbert to Julia Finch, Oct. 25, 1886, Gilbert Papers, LC.

10. Cass Gilbert to Julia Finch, Oct. 31 and Dec. 9, 1886, Mar. 2, 1887, Julia Finch to Cass Gilbert, Nov. 1, [1886], Gilbert Papers, LC. See Henry Van Brunt, "Henry Hobson Richardson, Architect," *Atlantic Monthly*, 58:349 (Nov. 1886), 685–93.

11. Cass Gilbert to Julia Finch, Dec. 10, 1886, Julia Finch to Cass Gilbert, Dec. 12, 1886, Gilbert Papers, LC.

12. Joseph M. Wells to Cass Gilbert, Dec. 12, 1886, Cass Gilbert to Julia Finch, Dec. 16, 1886, Gilbert Papers, LC.

13. Cass Gilbert to Julia Finch, May 15, 16, 1887, Gilbert Papers, LC.

14. Cass Gilbert to Julia Finch, June 11 and July 17, 1887, Gilbert Papers, LC.

15. Cass Gilbert to Julia Finch, Jan. 4 and Apr. 29, 1887, Julia Finch to Cass Gilbert, Mar. 1, 1887, Gilbert Papers, LC.

16. Cass Gilbert to Julia Finch, Jan. 4, July 15, 24, and Aug. 5, 1887, Julia Finch to Cass Gilbert, July 12, 15, Aug. 5, Sept. 14, 23, 1887. On the new popularity of apartment living in the late nineteenth century, see Gwendolyn Wright, *Building the Dream: A Social History of Housing in America* (Cambridge: MIT Press, 1981), Ch. 8. For a contemporary view of the relationship between apartment living and "the servant problem," see Robert Grant, *The Art of Living* (New York: Scribner's, 1895), 63–75.

17. Cass Gilbert to Julia Finch, June 3 and July 17, 1887, Julia Finch to Cass Gilbert, July 28, Aug. 3, 24, 1887, Gilbert Papers, LC.

18. Julia Finch to Cass Gilbert, Sept. 17, 23, and Oct. 11, 1887, Gilbert Papers, LC.

19. Cass Gilbert to Julia Finch, Nov. 16, 1887, Gilbert Papers, LC.

20. Cass Gilbert to Julia Finch, Nov. 14, 1887, Julia Finch to Cass Gilbert, Nov. 18, [1887], Gilbert Papers, LC.

21. Cass Gilbert to Elizabeth Gilbert, Nov. 24, 1887, Elizabeth Gilbert to Cass Gilbert, Nov. 30, 1887, Gilbert Papers, LC. For "quiet weddings," see Mrs. John Sherwood, *Manners and Social Usages* (New York: Harper, 1884), 128.

NOTES TO CHAPTER 7

1. Guy Kirkham, "Cass Gilbert, Master of Style," *Pencil Points*, 15:11 (Nov. 1934), 543, quoting a Gilbert letter of June 12, 1888. Kirkham may well have been the letter's recipient, since he had joined the office staff of Gilbert and Taylor at just that time.

2. Cass Gilbert to Julia Finch, Mar. 2, 11, and 22, 1887, Julia Finch to Cass Gilbert, Mar. 24, 1887, Gilbert Papers, LC.

3. Cass Gilbert to Julia Finch, May 8, June 3, and Nov. 15, 1887, Gilbert Papers, LC.

4. Cass Gilbert to Julia Finch, Oct. 9, 1887, Gilbert Papers, LC. For a good sketch of the history of the New York Life Insurance building in St. Paul, see Larry Millett, *Lost Twin Cities*, 212–14.

5. Robert Rantoul, "Memoir of William Endicott," *Massachusetts Historical Society Proceedings, 1914–15* (Boston: Massachusetts Historical Society, 1915), 48:243–52; Gilbert & Taylor to William Endicott, June 29 and Nov. 9, 1888, Gilbert Papers, MHS; Cass Gilbert to Julia Gilbert, May 15, 1889, Gilbert Papers, LC.

6. Cass Gilbert to Elizabeth Gilbert, Jan. 27, 1890, Gilbert Papers, LC.

7. Joseph Wells to Cass Gilbert, Nov. 6, 1889, Gilbert Papers, LC. A useful discussion of the Endicott Building appears in Sharon Irish, "West Hails East: Cass Gilbert in Minnesota," *Minnesota History*, 53:5 (Spring 1993), 201–4.

8. Cass Gilbert to Elizabeth Gilbert, Jan. 27, 1890, Daniel Burnham to Cass Gilbert, Sept. 21, 1889, Gilbert Papers, LC; Frank Bacon to Cass Gilbert, Oct. 30, 1890, Thomas Hastings to Cass Gilbert, Nov. 19, 1890, Gilbert Papers, MHS.

9. *Inland Architect and Building News*, 6:1 (Aug. 1885), 3; Charles King, "The Twin Cities of the Northwest," *Cosmopolitan*, 9:6 (Oct. 1890), 759; Schuyler, "Glimpses of Western Architecture."

10. Julia Gilbert to Cass Gilbert, Jan. 24, [1889], Gilbert Papers, LC; Cass Gilbert to Cooper Brass Works, Feb. 18, 1891, Cass Gilbert personal letterbook, Gilbert Papers, NYHS; Daniel Willard to Cass Gilbert, Mar. 6, 1891, Gilbert Papers, MHS.

11. Cass Gilbert to William Windom, Dec. 17, 1890, Cass Gilbert to James J. Hill, Dec. 20, 1890, Cass Gilbert personal letterbook, Gilbert Papers, NYHS; W. E. Curtis to Cass Gilbert, June 27, 1893, William Endicott to Cass Gilbert, July 11, 1893, Gilbert Papers, MHS.

12. Cass Gilbert to William Mead, Dec. 20, 1890, personal letterbook, Gilbert Papers, NYHS; William Mead to Cass Gilbert, Dec. 29, 1890, Gilbert Papers, MHS.

13. William Mead to Cass Gilbert, Jan. 19, 1891, Daniel Burnham to Frank Sickles, Jan. 31, 1891, Daniel Burnham to William Mead, Feb. 2, 1891, Cass Gilbert to Daniel Burnham, Feb. 18, 1891, Daniel Burnham to Cass Gilbert, Mar. 5, 23, 1891, Cass Gilbert to Charles McKim, Mar. 25, 1891, Gilbert Papers, MHS; Cass

Gilbert to Daniel Burnham, Mar. 24, 1891, personal letterbook, Gilbert Papers, NYHS; Cass Gilbert to Julia Gilbert, Mar. 5, 9, 1891, Gilbert Papers, LC; Charles Moore, *Daniel H. Burnham: Architect, Planner of Cities* (Boston: Houghton Mifflin, 1921), 48–49; Donald Hoffmann, *The Architecture of John Wellborn Root* (Baltimore: Johns Hopkins University Press, 1973), 182.

14. Cass Gilbert to Elizabeth Gilbert, Feb. 3, 1891, Gilbert Papers, LC; *Inland Architect and News Record*, 22:3 (Oct. 1893), 3; Moore, *Burnham*, 68, 85–86; Hoffmann, *Root*, 220.

15. Cass Gilbert to Editor, *Harper's Monthly*, May 3, 1891, Cass Gilbert to C. H. Walker, June 20, 1891, Cass Gilbert to "My Dear Willard," Oct. 7, 1891, Cass Gilbert to J. W. Stevens, Oct. 6, 1891, personal letterbook, Gilbert Papers, NYHS.

16. A handy biography is Stewart Holbrook, *James J. Hill: A Great Life in Brief* (New York: Knopf, 1955). Albro Martin, *James J. Hill and the Opening of the Northwest* (New York: Oxford, 1976) is a more detailed scholarly appraisal. For the impact of the Great Northern on the economic development of the region, see Elwyn Robinson, *History of North Dakota* (Lincoln: University of Nebraska Press, 1966), 227–30.

17. Information about the Grand Forks station, which survives much altered, has been provided by Sandra Slater, Head of Special Collections at the Library of the University of North Dakota.

18. Cass Gilbert to E. C. Simmons, June 4, 1907, Cass Gilbert Letterbook, OCA. John Thomas, *Alternative America: Henry George, Edward Bellamy, Henry Demarest Lloyd, and the Adversary Tradition* (Cambridge: Harvard University Press, 1983) includes an authoritative analysis of Single Tax doctrine. See also Geoffrey Blodgett, "Henry George and Utopia," in *American Reform and Reformers*, Randall Miller and Paul Cimbala, eds. (Westport: Greenwood Press, 1996), 242–54. Hamlin Garland's famous short story, "Under The Lion's Paw," in his *Main Travelled Roads* (Boston: Arena, 1891), effectively dramatized Henry George's animus against absentee landlords.

19. Cass Gilbert to Charles Gilbert, Oct. 11, 1890, Cass Gilbert personal letterbook, Gilbert Papers, NYHS.

20. Cass Gilbert to John Beverly Robinson, draft, Sept. 25, 1891, Gilbert Papers, MHS.

21. A sampling of attitudes toward labor troubles among Midwestern architects and contractors may be gained from *Inland Architect and News Record*—in particular, editorial comments in the issues of June 1887, Apr. 1888, June 1890, and June 1891. The latter issue includes a discussion of delays caused by union demands in the construction of buildings for the Chicago World's Fair, which opened a year behind schedule in 1893.

22. Robert D. Cross, *The Emergence of Liberal Catholicism in America* (Cambridge: Harvard University Press, 1958), 38–39.

23. Holbrook, *Hill*, 100; Martin, *Hill*, 452–53; Joseph Gilpin Pyle, *The Life of James J. Hill* (New York: Doubleday, Page and Co., 1917), 63–65.

24. Cass Gilbert Diary, Oct. 22–Dec 28, 1891, Gilbert Papers, LC.

25. Cass Gilbert Diary, Feb. 25, 1892, Gilbert Papers, LC; office memo dated Apr. 8, 1892, John Ireland to Cass Gilbert, Aug. 14, 28, 1894, Gilbert Papers, MHS; Cross, *Emergence of Liberal Catholicism,* 150.

26. Cass Gilbert to G. B. Rose, Oct. 4, 1933, Gilbert Papers, LC. Montgomery Schuyler identified "unity," "magnitude," and "illusion" as the keys to the fair's success. See his essay, "Last Words About the World's Fair," *Architectural Record*, 3

(Jan.–Mar. 1894), 271–301. See also David Burg, *Chicago's White City of 1893* (Lexington: University Press of Kentucky, 1976) and Stanley Appelbaum, *The Chicago World's Fair of 1893* (New York: Dover, 1980).

27. Sharon Irish, *Cass Gilbert's Career,* 43; Cass Gilbert to Julia Gilbert, Apr. 28, 1892, Mar. 6, 7, 1893, Halsey Ives to Cass Gilbert, Feb. 11, 1893, Gilbert Papers, LC.

28. Lansing Warner to Cass Gilbert, July 18, 1893, Charles Gilbert to Cass Gilbert, Mar. 13, 1894, May 16, 1894, and Oct. 21, 1895, Samuel Gilbert to Cass Gilbert, Sept. 19, 1893, Robert Peabody to Cass Gilbert, July 8, 1893, W. H. Hoffman to Cass Gilbert, Feb. 24, 1894, Gilbert Papers, MHS.

29. Cass Gilbert to Julia Finch, June 5, 1887, Gilbert Papers, LC; Neil Thompson, *Minnesota's State Capitol: The Art and Politics of a Public Building* (St. Paul: Minnesota Historical Society, 1974), 10. For Channing Seabury, see Albert N. Marquis, ed., *The Book of Minnesotans: A Biographical Dictionary* (Chicago: A. N. Marquis, 1907).

NOTES TO CHAPTER 8

1. The quotation is from Egon Verheyen, "'Unenlightened by a single ray from Antiquity': John Quincy Adams and the Design of the Pediment for the United States Capitol," *International Journal of the Classical Tradition*, 3:2 (Fall 1996), 215–16.

2. This summary, grounded in onsite photography by the author, also draws on a valuable analytical survey, Henry-Russell Hitchcock and William Seale, *Temples of Democracy: The State Capitols of the U.S.A.* (New York: Harcourt Brace Jovanovich, 1976), 17–203. See also Pamela Simpson, "Substitute Gimcrackery: Ornamental Architectural Materials, 1870–1930," *Ideas*, 5:1 (1997), 37–47.

3. Cass Gilbert, memorandum dated Apr. 26, 1886, Gilbert Papers, LC; Cass Gilbert to Mr. Whitney, Jan. 20, 1891, personal letterbook, Gilbert Papers, NYHS. For the Rhode Island capitol, see *American Architect and Building News*, 35:842 (Feb. 13, 1892).

4. Dankmar Adler to Cass Gilbert, Dec. 18, 22, 1891, Gilbert Papers, MHS. For a sympathetic view of the AIA's professional claims, see "Are We Just to Our Architects?" *Century*, 37:3 (Jan. 1889), 473–74.

5. Neil B. Thompson, *Minnesota State Capitol*, 8–12.

6. Channing Seabury to John De Laitre, Nov. 8, 1895; Channing Seabury to Charles Cole, June 19, 1896, box 3, Gilbert Papers, MHS.

7. Cass Gilbert to Board of Commissioners, Aug. 18, 1897, box 3, Gilbert Papers, MHS.

8. Cass Gilbert to F. C. Gibbs, Feb. 4, 1898, box 18, Gilbert Papers, MHS.

9. Cass Gilbert to Ralph Adams Cram, Dec. 31, 1907, Cass Gilbert personal letterbook, 1907, NYHS.

10. Thomas O'Sullivan, *North Star Statehouse: An Armchair Guide to the Minnesota State Capitol* (St. Paul: Pogo Press, 1994).

NOTES TO EPILOGUE

1. Cass Gilbert to Julia Finch, April 5, 1900, box 6, Gilbert Papers, LC.
2. Cass Gilbert to Charles Moore, Jan. 27, 1911, Gilbert Letterbook, OCA.
3. Cass Gilbert entry, n.d., 1932 Diary, box 1, Gilbert Papers, LC.

INDEX

Page numbers in italic refer to illustrations.
C refers to color plates following page 92.
Cass Gilbert is abbreviated CG.

Index

Index

Cass Gilbert: The Early Years was designed and set in type by Will Powers at the Minnesota Historical Society Press. The typeface is American Garamond, drawn by Morris Fuller Benton for American Type Founders Co., 1917–1919. This book was printed by the Maple Press Co., York, Pennsylvania.